THE COMPREHENSIVE BEGINNERS RUNNING GUIDE

A TOTAL RUNNING PLAN FOR LONG TERM GROWTH AND SUCCESS

JOSEPH GIORDANO

The information contained herein should not be construed as medical advice but should be used for informational purposes only. The information presented here should not be used to diagnose, treat, or cure any disease. In addition, it should not be used as a substitute for professional medical advice.

If you have any issues regarding your health or a medical condition, you should always consult your physician or another trained health expert. Never dismiss or put off obtaining competent medical advice because of something you've read in this book.

Table of Contents

Foreword

When I was twenty-one years old, I started my journey as a runner. It was in my junior year of college that I became good friends with one of my classmates, who was an avid runner and vegetarian. He and his wife were very health conscious, and because of their disciplined devotion to their healthy lifestyle and my nagging weight and allergy issues, I also became a vegetarian. At the time, I was a bit overweight. However, I discovered that the diet and exercise regimen I followed from that day forward was very helpful in enabling me to lose weight and eventually become an average weight for my body frame. I still do not glance in the rearview mirror, and despite the passage of several decades, I continue to adhere to a vegan diet and run three to four times per week.

Initially, I started running by myself but eventually joined my friend Vernon and his wife since it was less lonesome than running solo. My friend told me to stretch and do specific exercises before running constantly. For example, he taught me to do 5 to 10 minutes of walking lunges, hip flexor stretches, side stretches, and the hip circle exercise before running. These dynamic stretching exercises are beneficial as they work the quads, hamstrings, glutes, hip flexors, abs, back, and calves.

I recall that before running together with my friends, I did not correctly prepare before running. For example, I only spent a couple of minutes doing leg raises and leg stretches before starting a run. Unfortunately, I learned the hard way and suffered quite a bit from muscle strain and a pulled hamstring when first starting and had to stop running for over four weeks. Fortunately, after following my friend's sound advice by doing these exercises before I started running, I could properly work out various muscles throughout my body and avoid those same injuries.

From personal experience, I realize that the most challenging part of starting a running program is actually to start. Obviously, each one of us will have a unique set of factors that may prevent us from getting started. However, it is essential to know that approximately 50 million people are runners in the United States. Each of them started just where you are now, but they decided to take the first step. As you will read in this book, there are many benefits to starting a running program, and I hope you, too, will embark on this new journey.

When I first started, I did not have any goal projection of how many miles I wanted to run. I proceeded in small steps, and my initial goal was to run a 5K. This is a reasonable distance for a beginner to like to attain, and this length can be achieved in about two months of training. It took me about four months of training to be able to run a 5K due to a few minor injuries I experienced. Once I achieved a 5K, I became persistent in wanting to go further and then trained to run a 10K. I was able to complete a 10-kilometer run after training for six months. I did not stop there, and my achievements became infectious and trained and then achieved a 15K run one month later.

In high school and college, I enjoyed sports and took part in touch football, basketball, and softball. I certainly was not a gifted athlete but always admired those that were since they were so dedicated to keeping their bodies in such great shape. These athletes inspired me to go further with my running lifestyle, and after nine months of running, I completed a half marathon. Since I took things slowly, it took me quite a bit of time than most beginners to achieve a half marathon. Most beginner runners can complete a half marathon in three to four months. Those people who have previously been joggers can attain it in one to three months.

Being a New York native, I always followed the New York City Marathon. I remember in the late 1980's I used to attend the event as a spectator. Seeing these athletes run inspired me to want to achieve what they were doing. Since I have already completed a half marathon, I now set my sights on training to run a marathon. As a total newbie, it took me eleven months to train to run a marathon. I realize that it took me longer than most people to attain this, but I always took things slowly and cautiously to prevent injuries.

In 1992, for the first time, I entered the New York City Marathon. It was exhilarating to see the 3 million spectators cheering us on, inspiring us to reach the finish line. Since that year, I have entered the event fifteen times. Unfortunately, the last time that I entered the event was in 2019, and after that year, I stayed out of the event due to COVID.

I am telling you my story not to brag but to offer you confidence and inspiration because you, too, can achieve this. Just remember, it starts with the idea that you want to change your life by getting in shape and improving your health. So first, you should make an appointment with your doctor to see if you should start a running program at this time. Hopefully, the doctor will find you in excellent health, and you can now embark on this new lifestyle.

Do not be in a rush to reach the marathon mark but focus on one step at a time. For example, consider following a pattern of first wanting to attain a 5K and then proceeding to the next milestone. Once you achieve the next milestone, you will have the strength and determination to want to reach the next goal.

No matter how long it takes to achieve your objectives, it would help if you always were optimistic about this pursuit, and training for a marathon is one of those things. Besides enhancing your fitness and overall health, you may also acquire other beneficial attributes, such as determination, self-discipline, and confidence, which may be transferred to other aspects of your life and help you achieve your personal goals.

I hope my experience will give you the necessary push to get you started on a new and healthy way of living. Take things slowly, have self-compassion and persistence, and keep in mind that there is nothing that can prevent you from accomplishing the goals you have set for yourself.

Energie
BASF
BASF

INTRODUCTION

You've just entered the world of running; I hope you enjoy your stay! Running is not only a great way to get in shape but also a fun way to get to know your area and the surrounding natural environment. Running is a natural human activity that we have been doing for thousands of years, from when hunter-gatherers ran in the wild to the modern-day marathoners who run at career-high paces. Since running is so deeply rooted in our history as a species, practically anyone of any age can begin running and achieve their desired health and fitness levels. Meeting new people is another fantastic benefit of running.

In addition, there are a slew of intriguing advantages to running, including the following:

- Helps increase your energy levels
- Helps improve your mood
- Helps you have a better night's sleep
- Gives you more self-assurance and stamina
- Helps prevent health problems such as high blood pressure, diabetes, depression, and anxiety

Regardless of the motivation behind your decision to begin running, choosing this book is an excellent way to get started. To start your running regimen, all you need to do is put on your running shoes and head out the door. But it can be a more significant challenge to maintain the consistency required to step out the door daily.

On your journey as a runner, this book will act as a guide and aid you along the way. You'll find the following topics in this book:

- Advice on how to lay the groundwork for running
- A variety of running programs designed for novices
- Pointers on how to improve your running form to go farther and more quickly while minimizing the risk of injury

Consult with your primary care doctor before increasing the kilometers you run every week. The best way to start your adventure is to begin thinking like a runner from the beginning of your training since this will set the tone for the rest of your journey.

When you first start your running program, you will most likely experience sensations of enthusiasm and vigor about the new commitment you are making to yourself. These feelings will last for the duration of your running program. On the other hand, there is a good chance that you may run into challenges along the way, and overcoming them will put your desire to the test.

Runners frequently engage in various activities and strategies to keep their motivation up consistently. The first step for most runners is to sign up with a running group or search for a training partner. There is a wide variety of each form of running organization imaginable, and each one is geared toward serving the needs of a particular subset of runners. For example, there are organizations whose primary concentration is on the social aspect of running, groups whose primary focus is on training for a particular race, and even groups whose primary goal is running for the benefit of a charitable organization or a common cause. The population of runners includes examples of each of these types of groups.

Another common strategy is to jog while simultaneously listening to music. A good playlist is essential to keep your energy levels up while out for the long run. This is due to research that indicates music has a beneficial effect on mood and performance. However, remember that using headphones while running has a few benefits and potential issues. Because of this, you need to consider the matter before deciding whether or not you want to pursue this as a course of action. While running with headphones on, you're less able to notice changes in your surroundings, which could put your safety at risk. Taking part in this physically demanding activity comes with several severe downsides, including this one. Taking breaks from headphones and running without them daily could benefit your workouts. In addition, you may want to consider keeping a log of your progress.

You will better know how to enhance your running performance if you keep a training diary. Since it allows you to express the highs and lows of your running experience as they occur and will enable you to do it in real-time. This might aid you while you attempt to increase the performance of whatever you are working on. It is a beautiful testimonial to the work you have put in and is a lovely tribute to the hard work you have completed, which is an extra plus. Even if you don't feel like working out, you don't have to do anything special; instead, look at your past accomplishments and use that as motivation to get back into shape.

Ultimately, but certainly not least, filling your living area, place of work, and social media feeds with inspirational running quotations can be of great use. The remarks of other accomplished runners may be all you need to boost your confidence and keep you going. You may not need anything else.

For many people, running becomes less appealing as they become older. Unfortunately, this is the norm. How did we answer this question in our early twenties and thirties? Will I be able to deliver the same level of speed that I had when I was in my twenties and thirties? Is it true that running may negatively affect an older person's health more than positive? This does not mean that senior runners can't be active for the rest of their lives, even though they're more prone to problems like muscle strain and require more recovery after an injury than younger runners.

Running may not appeal to specific individuals because they have long believed it is a tedious and unappealing pastime. This perception may have been formed over a lengthy period.

It's possible that you were required to do it when you were younger as part of a rigorous pre-season training routine for another activity or that it was a punishment for engaging in another sport. Both of these scenarios are plausible. It's also possible that you can't get that dreadful mile out of your thoughts that you had to run in gym class. This could be the case.

So, if you're having trouble with these mental hurdles, remember that just asking yourself whether or not you can overcome them is an essential first step in committing to your running's success. If you successfully meet the challenge, you have already invested in the potential outcome of your running. This displays not only your concern but also that you are aware of the amount of work required in the future.

There seems to be no manner of getting around the undeniable fact that the initial few steps might, in all likelihood, prove to be complicated. But, on the other hand, if you take things slowly and pay attention to what your body is trying to tell you, you will likely come to enjoy the choice to start running in the end.

What Makes People Afraid to Run and Why

The fear that one will fall short of one's objectives is one of the major factors that lead some people to avoid running. Researchers reviewed the topic of fear in sport, exercise, and physical activity. The researchers concluded that fear originates from a weakened perspective of oneself, a restricted or nonexistent feeling of success, and a desire to avoid the psychological toll of failure. This is particularly true if you have experienced a significant loss in your life. People's low self-esteem is typically at the root of most frequent concerns about failing at running (which you have the power to change).

Other common phobias associated with running include the following:

Concern about the Opinions of Other People

An investigation of people's worries around physical activity found that respondents attributed their anxiety to how their parents and primary teachers interacted with them. These people spent their entire lives fearing what other people thought of them, especially if not treated with respect or ridiculed. These concerns surfaced at a young age and were difficult to dispel.

Concern that One Is Not Enough

Studying attitudes and barriers to exercise in people with type 1 diabetes found that humiliation and poor body image had a significant role in their decision to avoid exercising. They also claim that individuals who do not have diabetes face the same challenges while attempting to engage in physical activity.

Anxiety Regarding One's Safety

You may be afraid of running because you are concerned about your health or safety. The respondents in a research study on decisions affecting physical activity and exercise in people who survived breast cancer stated that the factors of safety and effectiveness influenced their choices. They will avoid the activity if they do not believe they are secure when running. In addition, concerns over one's physical safety are also warranted. A thorough grasp of the possible risks is vital, even if it is easy to "lace up your shoes and go. "Running by yourself can be nerve-wracking, especially if you do it early in the morning, late at night, or in an area with a lower population density. Running with a friend or in a group can alleviate some of these worries over the logistics of the situation.

How You Can Conquer Feelings of Fear and Intimidation

You can gradually move away from your anxieties, but this will not happen overnight or the following day. However, you can begin taking baby steps right now that will assist you in conquering such phobias, such as the following:

First, Maintain an Awareness of Your Present Circumstances

As stated by Harvard Health, mindfulness practice teaches you to keep your focus in the here and now rather than allowing it to wander into the past or the future. This helps you avoid overreacting to your anxieties and lessens the stress and despair from dwelling on those fears. You may maintain mindfulness by concentrating on the world around you, paying attention to your breathing, and pushing away any distracting thoughts that come into your head.

Meditate Regularly

Meditation is not difficult; all you need to do is close your eyes and sit in silence to meditate. When you feel anxious before beginning a run, you have two options: you may close your eyes and focus on a single thought that brings you comfort, or you can count your breaths and then start jogging. This has the potential to alter both your mentality and the way you act.

Imagine the World in Which You Wish to Live

Making use of one's imagination is one of the more common treatments for anxiety disorders, as the findings of a study that was only recently published on the subject in the journal Neuron suggest. They propose that imagination is beneficial in lowering threat-related brain patterns and physiological reactions from real-world threatening cues, such as the real worries you have about running. One example is how imagination can help you overcome your fears of running. For example, if you want to go for a run but are afraid about doing so, you may try envisioning yourself enjoying the run instead. This could help you overcome your anxiety and go for the run. Your way of thinking may shift significantly as a result of this.

Contributes to the Upkeep of a Healthy Body Weight

Running is a powerful kind of cardio exercise because it helps you burn a lot of calories. Running, as compared to walking, generates a more significant expenditure of energy, which, according to a study that was recorded in Medicine and Science in Sports and Exercise in 2013, makes it simpler to maintain a normal weight range, which is an essential component of healthy aging. If you are of advanced age and have a substantial amount of excess body fat, you significantly increase your likelihood of developing several health conditions, the most common of which are cardiovascular disease, high blood pressure, stroke, and diabetes.

Increases Bone Density and Joint Stability

Running exerts a lot of stress on the bones, which is why it's a great way to develop bone density. This is an important consideration to remember as you become older, as running increases the load on bones. Researchers examined knee discomfort and deterioration in runners with and without osteoarthritis in a study that was published in 2017 and covered ten years. Researchers have shown that consistent running helps strengthen joints and protect against knee osteoarthritis.

Improves Both the Lifespan and the Quality of life

As much as 23% to 30% decreased risk from all causes of death were found in a 2020 meta-analysis of more than 200,000 runners, according to researchers. This included a reduced risk of cardiovascular disease and cancer. The researchers concluded that running, even once a week, can significantly increase general health and longevity.

How to Rekindle Your Love of Running Back After It's Gone

Do you remember when you used to be a serious runner or a competitive athlete, but now you find that you have less time to spend being physically active? In addition, as you get older, your risk of injury increases, your recovery takes longer, and you have less energy overall. These are all excellent reasons to stop running. However, regaining your enthusiasm for running and being able to run well into your fifties, sixties, and even beyond may be feasible.

Take an optimistic outlook on life and create goals for yourself that are commensurate with your abilities. To get started, make sure your goals are manageable and start by not comparing yourself to other runners, especially those who are younger (or your younger self). Instead, it would help if you tried to accept where you are in life and concentrate on running because you enjoy it.

The positive effects that running will have on your physical and emotional health will serve as a source of inspiration for you, urging you to head outside and keep running.

Here are some safety precautions and motivational pointers for runners beyond 30.

Make New Goals Your Focus

Setting goals is an excellent method for changing unhealthy behaviors into healthier ones. Focus on the future and develop exciting new running goals to reignite your passion for the sport. Find an upcoming 5k race, and start training for it. An excellent method to keep yourself motivated is registering for a race in a different place. This allows you to arrange a trip and gives you something to look forward to.

Tune in to the Cues of Your Body

To avoid getting hurt, paying attention to the indications your body gives you is essential. Do not push yourself to exhaustion by forcing yourself to run on a day when you feel tired and stiff. If you are experiencing stiffness, poor energy, and a lack of motivation, you may suffer from overtraining syndrome. This can be diagnosed through a physical examination. If the alternative is becoming injured and unable to run the next day, taking a day off to recover and rest is preferable.

Honor and Commemorate Your Accomplishments

It is not necessary for the goals you set to be outcome-driven. For instance, you may commit to running five times a week for the next four weeks and then track your progress by crossing off the days on a calendar as you complete them. If you can maintain your running schedule for the entire month, you should reward yourself by attending a night out or doing something you have wanted for a long time. To maintain your motivation, you might want to consider rewarding yourself with a brand-new pair of running shoes or another piece of running gear.

Don't Forget to Get Warmed Up!

We are all aware that we should perform warming up before exercise and cool down afterward, but the question is: how many of us do it? These often-overlooked pursuits acquire a greater level of significance as we become older. Walking quickly for five minutes while also stretching can help you immediately get the most out of your training. After that, walk about for five minutes to cool down, and then stretch your hamstrings, quads, and calves to lessen the likelihood of muscle discomfort and damage.

Get Yourself Checked Out Thoroughly

Before running, you should make an appointment for a checkup with your primary care physician. Talk to your doctor about your plans to run and find out if there are any health risks you should be aware of, such as high blood pressure, diabetes, or joint problems.

How to Maintain Your Motivation: Some Tips

Fear is something that can always come back once you've started running. However, taking steps to prevent this from occurring can assist you in maintaining your motivation and keeping you engaged in the sport.

Choose to Go for a Brief Walk.

If you are still experiencing fear, you do not have to go outside and run; instead, you can go for straightforward, thoughtful walks. Pay attention to your body awareness, breathing, and environment around you while on these walks. For example, people who participated in a study and walked mindfully for thirty minutes twice a week for one month reported feeling less stressed and having a higher quality of life overall.

Employ a Competing Running Coach.

You can work with a running coach who focuses on novice athletes. A coach may evaluate your present fitness level, determine your strengths, and devise a training plan that will assist you in achieving the running goals you have set for yourself. You are free to discuss your concerns with the coach and get help working through them with someone with years of relevant experience.

Running is beneficial on many levels for people of all ages and levels of physical fitness. You can improve your cardiovascular health, prolong your longevity, maintain healthy body composition, increase your cognitive ability, and improve your mental health. However, it is not a simple effort to incorporate running into your routine and make that change. Modifying your frame of mind is the first and most crucial step. You will never be motivated to run if you see the activity as a responsibility to be fulfilled. Consider running not only a means to an end but also a means to a respite from the stresses of the day, a reward for a body that has labored so hard for you during the day, and an activity that merits a prize after it has been completed.

CHAPTER 1

Why It Is Critical for All Runners To Have A Growth Mindset

When you achieve something, you should celebrate, but when you don't, you should try to figure out why. A cliche, but there's some truth behind it, just like many other cliches. Runners who cultivate a "growth mentality" can get the most out of races and training runs that do not go according to plan by allowing these experiences to contribute to and guide future decisions.

Carol Dweck, a psychologist, is the one who came up with the concept of having a development mindset. It all boils down to how you look at yourself in the most basic terms possible. Do you think that your talents and skills can never be improved, or do you think you can get better if you put in the work and pay attention to what you're doing?

How do you respond when a race does not go as planned? The wheels may have come off at mile 20 of a marathon, or perhaps you picked up an injury that forced you to stop running. On the other hand, it's possible that you didn't even make it to the starting line because of an ailment. How did you react when you encountered these obstacles? Did you try to convince yourself that you were worthless? It's possible that you said something like, "I'll go back to my favorite distance; that's exactly why I don't run marathons (or whatever)."

Our tendency to retreat to our safe space and avoid situations that force us out of our comfort zone indicates that we have a fixed attitude. When you have a growth mentality, you are willing to accept the risk of failing, and you recast failure as an essential building block for future success. If you experience failures, you will have plans to learn from them and improve in the future.

It is necessary to put your body through strain to create progress.

You will be better once you have rested and adapted to this tension. When you adopt a growth mentality, you will be prepared to put yourself in stressful situations, push yourself to your limits, and improve your fitness. Having a growth mindset helps you remain focused on achieving success and the processes involved in doing so.

Instead of being an exam that must be passed or failed, every race or session is an opportunity to learn something new. A positive mindset directs your attention not just to the achievement of accomplishment but also to the processes involved in achieving that success. This has the potential to benefit from lessening the stress levels associated with racing, as you will be less focused on the outcome alone; instead, you will be just as interested in the process and what it may tell you about yourself. In a nutshell, having a growth mindset is a method that can help you manage the tension and anxieties that many runners experience before a race.

If you have a growth mentality, you will look at any setback, such as falling short of a goal, as merely an opportunity to improve. You take time to think things over and develop a new strategy. For example, perhaps you need to switch up your workout routine to include additional strength training, or you could try a new system for pacing or fueling. As you make these changes, you will become a better and more prepared athlete, and you will see evidence of this improvement in both the outcomes of your races and your overall performance. But it isn't enough to merely say that you "believe in yourself" - It's not just a matter of having a positive frame of mind. The focus here is on conducting methodical introspection.

Work and effort are necessary components of a growth mentality.

The first step is as follows. A growth mentality is a coping mechanism that can be used to manage the tension and anxieties many runners experience before a race.

1. Establish a starting point.

If you don't have a baseline to compare your new results, measuring your improvement will be tough. Spend time thinking about where you are in your training and where you want to be at the beginning of each training block.

Give this a try: I give each of my athlete friends a simple score out of ten on a spreadsheet and ask them to self-evaluate their current capabilities and areas in which they may improve. It addresses various topics, including physical fitness, psychological health, lifestyle choices, and recovery strategies. In each case, we note methods to improve things in the short, medium, and long terms.

2. Consider the past.

A growth mentality is driven by introspection of oneself. Spend some time thinking about what aspects of your racing and training have been successful and what factors could use some tweaking so that you can learn more.

Give this a try: Maintain a detailed training diary, in which you write down your thoughts and observations regarding your training. It's not just about how long or how fast you ran; it's also about how you felt and what you were thinking while doing it. Noting what method of pace and nutrition works best for you, as well as what your stress levels were and how well you have been recuperating, will help you develop a rich supply of relevant data.

3. Start Thinking Big.

If you only give yourself tasks that you are confident you can complete, it will be tough to advance in your career. We have a propensity to alleviate the pressure we are under by lowering our standards and restricting our goals. It isn't always about going for a long-distance; maybe you want to focus on getting faster over shorter distances or try to compete in cross-country races, mountain races, or trail races instead.

Give this a try: Being ambitious is not the same as being irresponsible; the goals you set for yourself should challenge you without causing you to fail. So, if you want to go further or aim for a significant increase in speed, make sure you give yourself enough time to get there without becoming exhausted.

4. Expand your view of the world around you

Establish several success measurements,' going beyond merely paces or personal bests, encompassing 'process' goals for your training and racing, and put these into action.

Give this a try: Think about approaching competitions with a different frame of mind.

"Today, success will be evaluated by keeping to my fueling plan," "I'll race without a watch and strive to manage my own perceived effort," and "Today, success will be defined by a negative split." These present learning possibilities that are not available if one concentrates on a predetermined number displayed on a watch.

5. Be eager for comments and criticisms.

Do you cringe at the thought of being criticized? If this is the case, you could very well be stifling any potential for expansion. Find occasions where you can collect input and hear a variety of perspectives.

Give this a try: You might want to consider becoming a member of a nearby club and discussing your running and training with the head coach there. If you cannot do this, you should get together with a group of your running friends and discuss your individual training goals. This will allow you to produce new ideas and receive constructive criticism.

6. Let yourself 'fail' on purpose

If you are not willing to take the chance of failing, it isn't easy to know what your boundaries are.

Give this a try: If you want to do something risky, look for a low-key event or park run to participate in. Try starting faster or running with runners you wouldn't ordinarily try to run with. Be willing to accept any outcome; if you find that you need to slow down or quit, you will be much closer to comprehending the boundaries of your current abilities.

7. Implement change

Instead of only recording and reflecting, come up with a plan of action to go forward.

Give this a try: Set up "review meetings" with yourself every four to six weeks at regular intervals. Consider both your plan and the progress you've made in your training. Are you making the kind of headway that you want to? If not, what modifications are required? Keep your action plan up to date, and maintain your dedication to making constant improvements.

8. Make sure to mix up your workouts.

The most glaring manifestation of a fixed attitude in runners is that we have a propensity to like and revel in the activities at which we are already skilled. If you continue to perform the same workouts weekly, you should not be surprised when you reach a plateau in your progress.

Give this a try: As your training gets more advanced, you need to ensure that you are giving yourself opportunities for diversity. What are you doing to give your mind and body something new to stimulate them? Alter not only the surfaces you train on but also the people you train with, the routes you run, and the sessions you include in your schedule.

Have you ever thought of something or spoken something that could be interpreted as "I go running, but I'm not a runner yet"?

Why do people who regularly engage in the activity of running try to distance themselves as far as possible from the label of "runner"?

Maybe we're afraid of the criticism from other people that we might receive once we start acting in our role as runners. Others can refer to you as "slow," "a jogger," or "not there yet" instead of praising your day-to-day commitment to succeed.

On the other hand, if you run, you already qualify as a runner. Along your path, some people may try to put you in your place, which may make you feel disheartened.

It may not be easy to believe that you are genuinely a runner due to the comments that others have made about your running ability.

To advance as a runner, you must first take joy in your running.

It makes no difference in how fast or how far you are going. Whenever you run, you are a runner.

You will be interfering with the activities of anyone using their leisure time to sit on the couch and watch television. You will be doing this if you put on your shoes and head outside (or get on the treadmill).

It's possible that you're interested in developing your running skills by reading this book. Or perhaps you want to find ways to make constant running a part of your routine and are looking for suggestions.

It may be challenging to begin incorporating running into your life if you haven't previously made it a regular part of your routine.

How do you get started running and keep it up in a way that will provide results that will stay for a long time? The first thing you need to do is convince yourself that you can run.

The following step is to determine where your mindset can be enhanced.

Follow these pointers to develop the mindset of a runner:

1. Begin with a two-minute countdown.

When beginning a new activity, such as running, you should strive to make the process as straightforward and uncomplicated as possible. It will be easier to start showing up for your workouts if your first sessions are limited to two minutes each. This will allow you to transition more easily into your usual pattern of going for a run.

2. Transform your goal into a concrete plan of action.

Run as if you are doing it because you want to, rather than because it is something you are obligated to do. Consider the activity of running as something you look forward to doing to persuade your brain to continue with the strategy.

3. Slow progress does not equate to "not making any progress."

Learn to be content with progress rather than perfection. You shouldn't expect to shatter your records immediately. If you feel disheartened, it can be helpful to remind yourself that even the most minor steps ahead are still stepped forward. Keep in mind that any forward motion is welcome!

4. Tenacity is just as vital as progress.

Your commitment to attaining your goals is equally as crucial as your established groundwork. Finding the determination to get up and go through with your daily routine might be challenging. But, recognize that you are committed to showing up and going for the run.

5. Reward yourself after every triumph, no matter how minor it may have been.

Your brain may be trained to look forward to running if you give yourself rewards after each mile when you complete a milestone; whether something as simple as walking outdoors or something more challenging, be sure to have a gift waiting for you. There will be occasions in which you will, for whatever reason, feel unmotivated to run, and these periods are inevitable. It's possible that this is happening because you're pushing yourself to the edge of your physical capabilities. There is also the possibility that running, because of the repeated nature of the action that it entails, serves as a cerebral workout in addition to being a physical exercise.

You will always have your mindset to rely on, even when you feel unmotivated and start having doubts about who you are as a person.

Remember the following:

> Even though we are making slow progress, we are nonetheless making progress.
>
> You have the determination to show up and run, even if that decision hasn't been made yet (even if that decision isn't today).
>
> Every triumph is a success in and of itself (even the small ones).

It is essential to be there, even if only for a minute or two. Simply making an appearance is a step in the right direction. As you get better at controlling your thinking, you may start to manage your foundation better.

6712
DOURO
6639
DOURO

CHAPTER 2

Essential Tips for Building a Solid Foundation for Beginner Runners

It seems inappropriate to begin a new year without first discussing one's aspirations and promises to oneself. Beginning a regimen is always a popular choice for a New Year's resolution, whether the goal is to get healthier generally or to shed some pounds. On the other hand, many people try to do too much too quickly and wind up becoming injured or exhausted, which leads them to quit jogging altogether. On the other hand, that won't be you!

If you want to start running, stay injury-free, progress toward your goals, and enjoy the miles you put in.

There are no trade secrets; instead, there are a few basic tactics that might be of assistance to anyone interested in getting started.

1. Begin with alternating bouts of running and walking.

There is no reason to be concerned, even if the thought of jogging nonstop for one mile or three miles strikes fear in your heart. Interval training, in which you alternate between jogging and walking, is a tried-and-true strategy for developing a lifetime habit of running.

Intervals of running and walking are the safest and most effective approach to ease into running without risking injury or overtaxing your body to the point where you give up before settling into a pattern. Running stresses your muscles, bones, and joints in addition to working out your cardiovascular system. Running also strengthens your cardiovascular system.

Regardless if you have a decent cardiovascular fitness level due to doing the elliptical, spinning, or another activity that does not include running, take brief timed walk breaks. In contrast, your run will keep you from overstressing your musculoskeletal system. You'll lower your chances of getting common problems like runner's knee, shin splints, and IT band syndrome, and if you can avoid getting hurt while running, you'll be able to keep going for longer. Intervals of running and walking help you manage the effort you put into your run.

Running is challenging, but every run does not have to be (and in fact, shouldn't be) an all-out assault on your body. Take several breaks to walk around and regulate your breathing and pace so that you aren't huffing and puffing towards the end of the activity. Intervals of running and walking are easy to perform.

You may keep track of the time using the Runkeeper app on your smartphone, and you should break up a run that lasts for 20 to 30 minutes into several shorter rounds of running and walking (you can set this up in the app as fast and slow intervals).

Your current fitness level will determine the duration of the run intervals and the walk intervals in this workout.

People who have never exercised before should begin by running for 30–60 seconds, then walking for 1 minute. People who already have a solid physical foundation from participating in other sports or hobbies can begin their workouts by alternating between jogging for two to four minutes and walking for one minute. It would help if you gradually cut down the time you spend walking between your running intervals or lengthen the time you spend running until you can run without stopping.

2. Don't overdo it on the speeding.

Just running doesn't mean you have to give it your all every time. Running has the most significant health benefits and is the most fun when done at a moderate intensity. Even though you will exert more effort than you would if walking, you should strive to run at a speed where you can still communicate if necessary without being out of breath. You want to complete the race with the sensation that you could keep going for at least a few more minutes.

Easy can also refer to the number of times you run and the total amount of work you put in during your workouts. To get started, try running a week thrice for 20 to 30 minutes or alternating between jogging and walking. Going for a run every day is unnecessary, especially when you are initially getting started. Find out more about how to maintain the ease of your easy miles.

3. Be sure to eat appropriately both before and after your workout.

If you start running, you should avoid doing so on an empty stomach. This is true even if your goal is to exercise to reduce weight. Running burns a lot of calories, and your body can acquire that energy from carbohydrates as well as fat.

If you don't eat anything for a couple of hours before going for a run, your blood sugar may be low, which can make you feel sluggish and even lead you to pass out during your workout. There is no need to gorge yourself before your run; doing so may even create stomach discomfort while you are out on the trail. Consume a light meal high in carbohydrates about sixty to ninety minutes before you leave the house. You can get the required amount of energy for your run from a banana, a handful of raisins, or a slice of toast made with whole wheat flour, which won't weigh you down.

You must eat within the first hour after finishing your run and it is recommended that you do so. Your muscles are ready to replace the carbohydrates that they have burned, and by refilling these carbohydrate stores (glycogen), you are preparing your body for the next run that you will be doing. Additionally, your muscles require protein to repair themselves after you've gone for a run. In addition, eating after a run will help you control your appetite and prevent you from experiencing feelings of extreme hunger later on.

Aim for a light snack after your run, or better yet, get your workout in before a regular lunch. To speed up the healing process, load up on nutritious foods like lean protein, fruit, vegetables, and whole grains. When you first start running, there is no requirement for you to consume anything before, during, or after your runs. Shakes and other sports nutrition meals are not necessary for runs that last less than seventy-five to ninety minutes. Especially if you are eating a healthy diet that includes complex carbs, your muscles can store enough glucose in the form of glycogen to keep you running for a period that is shorter than 90 minutes.

4. Keep a training log

It is helpful to have a training partner or a coach to keep you accountable, but in the end, you are the only person who can hold you to your goals.

Because you can keep track of your development and evaluate how far you have gone, a training diary is an essential tool for each beginner runner to have. You are more likely to continue running and push yourself a little bit further each week if you can look back over the preceding month and see that you have made discernible progress.

If you utilize it on every run, the Runkeeper app can serve as a log for your workouts; therefore, you should be sure to track it each time you run. After the run, you will have the opportunity to evaluate your performance on past runs and discover new distance or pace bests that you made. Be careful to take down exactly how you were feeling at the time by using the notes functionality of the app. The app will tally up your monthly mileage, and it will display clear advancement as you continue to run more and more.

5. Start by laying down a solid foundation.

Your priority should be strengthening your foundation before competing in races or running great distances. This indicates that before beginning training for a half marathon or marathon, you should first wait until you have completed a minimum of six months of running (or run-walking) as a base activity. Your musculoskeletal system needs time to adjust to the physiological demands of running.

The first few months of your running regimen are the most critical time for this adaptation. You can lessen the likelihood of suffering an injury in the future by devoting a few months to forming a consistent running regimen, working to strengthen your muscles and joints, and establishing an aerobic base.

6. Invest in the avoidance of injuries.

When it comes to running injuries, having a solid core, hips, and glutes will assist you in avoiding being hurt as much as possible. You can perform strength training using weights or try out these straightforward exercises in the comfort of your own home. Start with one set of each exercise consisting of ten repetitions. If you do them either after a run or on days when you are not running, you will make significant progress toward becoming a more powerful runner.

Glute bridges

Position yourself so that you are lying on your back with your knees bent and your feet on the floor close to your butt. To form a straight diagonal line from your knees to your shoulders, squeeze your glutes and raise your hips as high as you comfortably can. Your torso should be in this position. Maintain a level hip position. After pausing, begin lowering yourself down carefully to finish one repetition.

Side-lying leg raises

Position yourself so that you are lying on your right side, with your knees bent and your feet planted firmly on the floor. Stack your shoulders, hips, and knees. Your body must be aligned in a straight line. You can support your head by propping it up with your right hand or resting it on your right arm. After raising your left leg as high as you comfortably can without causing instability in your hips or torso, please pause and then bring it back down to the starting position to complete one repetition. First, do all the repetitions on your right side, then move on to your left side.

Forearm plank

After getting into an elevated push-up position, lower yourself until resting on your forearms. The line formed by your body should be straight. Keep your abdominal muscles engaged by drawing your navel toward your spine, clench your glutes, and hold the plank position for thirty seconds.

One of the most challenging steps to take while beginning to run is the initial step outside the door. You shouldn't feel like you have to rush out of the starting gate. If you start running, it is best to take things at a more leisurely pace so that you can eventually cover more ground. Taking the effort to establish a solid base that will bring long-term happiness and protect against long-term harm is time well spent. This chapter will cover what you can do before, during, and after your runs so that you may get the most out of them.

Before you start running:

1. Set a goal.

Establish a purpose for your running practice, whether your objective is to complete your first 5 kilometers or your first 42 kilometers. Please put it in writing so you may refer back to it whenever you need a reminder of why you started running in the first place.

2. Take into consideration the advantages.

Are you aware that studies suggest that reminding yourself of the benefits of fulfilling your goals can lead to lasting changes? What are some of the advantages of reaching your running goals? You may feel more confident, have more energy, and perhaps lose weight.

3. Stretch.

Stretching your legs and the rest of your body before going for a run will help prevent injuries.

- **Lunges.**

Assume a split stance with your feet, and your right foot positioned around two to three feet in front of the left foot. Your core is engaged, your shoulders are back and down, and your hands are resting on your hips. Your torso is straight.

1. Knees should be bent, and the torso should be lowered so that the back knee is just a few inches from the ground. You want your front thigh to be parallel to the floor and your back knee to point

toward the ground when you reach the bottom of the exercise. In addition, while doing this exercise, your weight should be equally distributed between your legs.

2. Continue to retain your weight on the front foot's heel as you push yourself back up to the starting position.

   Your quadriceps, hamstrings, glutes, and core will benefit from making lunges, which is a great way to get ready for a run. Before and after your run, you should perform a few sets of lunges.

- **Pigeon posture.**

In yoga, pigeon posture, or eka pada rajakapotasana as it is known in Sanskrit, extends the hip flexors and lower back. On the ground, with one leg back and the other knee front, your upper body should be straight, and your hips should be rooted to the earth.

Your hips will feel more open when you try this stance. When you run, having a more excellent range of motion in your hip flexors helps you develop momentum. Injuries and soreness to the hip flexors that might be caused by running are also reduced due to this. It is a good idea to make the pigeon stance part of your warm-up and cool-down routine before and after you run.

- **Deep squat.**

A squat is considered to be deep when, at the deepest point of the movement pattern, the height of the squatter's hips is lower than the height of the squatter's knees. To put it another way, the angle formed by your knee joint in its most bent position is larger than one hundred degrees.

Squatting will help you develop more hip flexibility. Try it out! Your overall flexibility and the crucial muscles required for running will improve as a result of this activity.

4. Get your heart rate up with some gentle cardio.

The expansion of your heart, caused by warming up, enables it to handle the increased blood flow that results from jogging. Before you run, warm up with some easy aerobics to get your heart rate up. High knees are the ideal warm-up activity to perform before jogging. In addition, you can ease into running by beginning with brisk walking instead of running at first.

While you are in motion:

1. Bring your attention to your breathing.

Take a breath in via your nose, and then release it out of your mouth. Run at a pace that allows you to easily maintain control of your breathing while just getting started with running. You'll be able to run for longer period without experiencing cramps if you do this.

2. Pay attention to your bodily cues.

Make it a goal not to overdo it with your efforts. Find a running pace at which you can still carry on a conversation while doing it. Put yourself through increasingly complex challenges as you climb the ranks.

3. Pay attention to your form.

Your ability to run for longer lengths of time and the overall quality of your workouts will increase if you pay attention to your form. Put pressure on your shoulders to bring them down and back, and then drive your pelvis forward. You'll discover that it's challenging to learn how to focus on your breath, form, and body all at the same time while you're running, so be patient with yourself! For this reason, taking things gently at first is essential, and concentrating on getting the fundamentals down pat.

After running:

1. Stretch.

Once more, stretching out after you've finished running is the most effective strategy to prevent injuries. After completing your run, stretch using the pigeon position, hip circles, and lunges.

2. Take a deep breath.

After finishing your run, gradually slow down your heart rate. Take your breaths in and out more slowly, or finish your run with a short stroll to cool down. Relaxing your muscles and reducing their tension both help you stretch out after you cool down.

3. Be sure to record your accomplishments as you go.

Everything that can be measured can be managed. You'll have a better idea of where you stand on your objective if you keep regular records of your runs. Always ensure you have a firm grasp on the fundamentals before moving on to more complex strategies.

Building a foundation will, in general, assist you in preventing injury, which will allow you to continue making improvements and enjoy your runs. You can teach yourself to push your body's limitations and demonstrate to yourself that you can do anything you set your mind to if you learn to establish goals and listen to your body simultaneously.

CHAPTER 3

Discovering the Best Running Plan for Newbies

You have determined that running a 10-kilometer race at some point during this year would be fun. Maybe your objective for the moment is to finish two runs per week. In either event, you are prepared to get out onto the streets or trails for a run and to join the millions of other individuals who incorporate running into their routine training routines.

Before beginning any running program, Monica Betchker, PT, DPT, and AT, recommends discussing your running goals with your primary care physician. This is the best way to ensure that your running goals are realistic. Experts will examine to see if you are medically able to begin a running program and will help you identify any potential barriers that may develop along the road. They will also help you determine whether or not you are ready to begin a running program.

The following is a guide that will educate you on how to get started running and what information you need to know to do it safely and effectively.

Take care in making your shoe selection.

A reliable pair of shoes is the most crucial piece of equipment a runner may possess. Your selection of a running shoe can have a sizeable influence on the degree of comfort you experience during your workouts and the risk that you will develop an injury. You should go to a store that offers sporting goods or running shoes and ask to speak with a shoe expert to get a pair of shoes that suit your feet. This will allow you to get the most out of your purchase.

It is essential to select the type of footwear you put on so that it is compatible with how your foot hits the ground. These professionals will have you run for a few minutes on a treadmill or a smaller track so that they can evaluate your gait. This might take place either indoors or outdoors. Additionally, there are shoes designed specifically for running. There are strict rules on wearing regular walking shoes, cross-trainers, or trail shoes. It is essential to make the necessary investments of both time and effort to acquire suitable footwear.

If you wear orthotics or shoe inserts, you should always try on new shoes while you are wearing them to get the most accurate fit possible. There is also the option of purchasing additional inserts that can help absorb impact on other parts of your body, such as your knees and hips. These inserts are available for purchase on their own.

You should also make a point to remember to replace your shoes every four to six months or every 300 to 500 miles, whichever comes first. Of course, this recommendation is contingent on how frequently you run. Dress so that you may make the best possible first impression.

Runners should give lots of care to the gear that they wear for a variety of different reasons, including making sure that they are comfortable and being able to control their body temperature regardless of the weather outside. If the temperature is high and the humidity is high, you should dress in lighter-colored clothing that is less heavy and can wick away moisture. You will continue to have a lower body temperature due to this. If it is substantially colder, as well as if it is freezing and rainy, you should dress in three layers of clothing.

For you to remain unaware that you are sweating, the layers of clothes that are in direct contact with your skin must have the ability to wick away moisture from your body. The insulation you use, whether it is fleece, wool, or down, should be included in your intermediate layer. The outerwear that you wear should be water and wind-resistant, as this is the third and last outer layer that you should wear.

Wearing clothes that are light in color and, if possible, reflective is a good safety practice in general. It doesn't matter if it's the middle of the day or the middle of the night: drivers, especially those behind the wheel of huge vehicles like SUVs or trucks, can have difficulty finding you. When vehicles are around corners, or there's a change in the signal at a crosswalk, pedestrians are at the greatest danger of being struck by cars.

Running will also be a more pleasant experience for women if they wear a supportive sports bra, which is a notion that some people might consider self-evident.

Start Out with a Walk-Run Routine

To get started, you should put the walk-run routine through its paces. The run-walk technique is helpful for the overwhelming majority of individuals. It would help if you began by walking regularly, then work your way up to walking at a quick pace so that you may gradually build up your tolerance to the action of jogging. Eventually, you should be able to run. This is the most effective technique to start running if you have never done so.

When you are just starting out walking or running, it is best to refer to the amount of time spent in these activities in minutes rather than in kilometers. Beginning an exercise routine with intervals of one minute of running followed by two minutes of walking for a total of twenty to thirty minutes is a good place to start. After that, start by running for five minutes, and then during the following four weeks, add thirty seconds to that cumulative time until you reach ten minutes. Of course, this concept is open to modification depending on a person's overall health and the amount of fitness they already possess.

Even somebody who is physically able to conduct cardiovascular activity should enter into running slowly so that their bodies can adapt to the effects of running. Running may significantly impact a person's body, and it's essential to give it time to adjust. It would help if you exercised between three and four times per week, but not on back-to-back days. It would help if you began progressively increasing the time you spend running by a few minutes every week once you have reached 10 minutes of continuous running and no longer need to break up your runs with walking. When you have reached this milestone, you no longer need to walk throughout your runs. Carry on in this manner until you have reached the destination after traveling the necessary time or distance. In addition, the length of your runs does not need to be the same for every one of them. Alternating between shorter and longer distances while running, as well as including cross-training in your program, can help reduce the risk of injuries that can be sustained while running.

Be sure to keep yourself adequately nourished and hydrated while on your runs. Ensure you drink enough water while you're out there since this is another thing you can do to guarantee that your runs will go off without a hitch. Always drink water before, during, and after your workout to keep yourself hydrated and prevent dehydration from setting in. Even if the temperature is lower, it is still possible to become dehydrated due to the lack of moisture in the air.

The American College of Sports Medicine recommends that active persons drink at least 16 to 20 ounces of fluid within one to two hours before engaging in any outside activity. This will help to reduce the likelihood that they will become dehydrated during their participation in the activity. After that, while you are outside, you need to make sure you drink between 6 and 12 ounces of liquids every 10 to 15 minutes. This will help prevent dehydration. After taking part in the exercise, you must drink even more water than you did before.

It is recommended that you consume between 16 and 24 additional ounces per day to make up for your lost weight (2- 3 cups). Although water is the best option, many sports drinks can replace fluids and electrolytes like salt and potassium that are lost via sweat. So, again, water is the best option. The wisest choice is to drink water. If the amount of sodium and potassium in the body is too high or too low, this could potentially lead to health complications. The excruciating muscle cramps you've been experiencing may be due to an electrolyte deficiency.

However, suppose a runner wants to be adequately hydrated. In that case, they should avoid caffeinated and alcoholic liquids like coffee, tea, colas, and beer and wine. Dehydration can occur due to these fluids since they tend to suck water out of the body. The consumption of fruit juice and drinks has been linked to an increased risk of gastrointestinal distress due to their potentially high carbohydrate and low sodium content.

Log your miles

Keep a log of the distance you run as well as how you feel while you are out on your run Irrespective of whether or not your objective is to run a 5k or take part in a local event, it would be beneficial for you to bear this in mind because it would be valuable to you. Running is an excellent activity that can help you keep your current fitness level. You will need to construct your weekly base mileage and build weekly off of that if you are training for an event that is longer in distance, such as a half-marathon or a marathon. Likewise, you will need to do this if you are preparing for an event longer than 5k.

It is very beneficial to keep a log that tracks how you feel before, during, and after each run, in addition to the distance or amount of time you have run. This is especially useful for novices because it can help them identify areas in which they struggle and motivate them to do better. When you first start, you should make an effort to avoid running on consecutive days whenever possible. On days when you don't run, your body has the opportunity to repair itself and get stronger.

If you want to run successfully, a significant amount of rest is required. At least once every week, it would help if you stopped running to give your body the rest it needs. This will help you prevent injuries and exhaustion, which may be caused by increasing the mileage you are running. Increasing the mileage that you are running will help you avoid injuries. Consider taking an extra day off if you feel too exhausted to work, if you are unwell, or if you are experiencing discomfort in your muscles. Also, just because you have an unexpected day off doesn't mean you should add an extra day to your schedule.

After finishing workouts that are longer or more strenuous, it is a good idea to give yourself a day off or take it easy and let your muscles recover. If you are training for a race that is longer than a marathon, the last of your long runs should be completed approximately three weeks before the race. Several studies have concluded that muscle damage might occur after a highly rigorous workout for over three weeks straight.

Participation in a Marathon

You have signed up to participate in your first marathon, and preparations have begun. Before beginning training for a marathon, you should have established a consistent running routine that has lasted for at least a year. Most programs start with a basic mileage of between 20 and 25 miles per week at the very beginning. By utilizing this form as the base, the likelihood of you being having an injury is reduced significantly. You should aim for a training routine that lasts for a total of 18 weeks if you already have a strong foundation in the running.

Before commencing this routine, you should have covered a distance of at least five miles during one of your longest runs. It is generally agreed that the endurance work needed as part of the training is of the utmost importance. As a direct result of completing this exercise, your muscles, heart, and lungs will be conditioned to work effectively for extended periods. Running longer distances interspersed with shorter outings will assist you in gradually working up to longer distances. Choose the day of the week you will go for your long run.

Based on your average weekly mileage, the number of injuries you've experienced in the past, and your current level of running competence, you should be able to estimate the number of miles you should run on the remaining days of each week. During the first few weeks of the training program, a beginner who wants to run a marathon should get themselves ready to run a total of approximately 20 to 25 miles, and they should call themselves prepared to run up to 40 miles during the long runs, which are the long distances that are covered during the training program.

Because there are so many various entry points into the sport of running, it is not always easy to figure out where to begin when you are just beginning the sport for the first time. Do you start running? How can you improve your running so that it helps you reach your goals?

You can follow a running strategy designed for beginners. You'll feel more organized as a result, making it much simpler for you to go out the door. You won't have to spend any mental energy considering what you want to do during the day because all you have to do is lace up your running shoes, head outside, and start jogging.

Here are three training schedules for novice runners that you can follow.

7-Week Walking Plan

It is best to prepare your body for running by beginning with a regimen that involves walking for seven weeks. Although there are various iterations of the plan, the overall objective is to walk anywhere between 100 and 185 minutes per week.

It would help if you began slowly during the first week and then progressively increase the time you spend walking until you reach or exceed the maximum amount of time recommended.

1. On Monday, go for a 15- to 20-minute walk.
2. On Tuesday, go for a 25 to 40-minute walk.
3. Wednesday.

Get some rest or go for a walk for 15 to 20 minutes.

4. On Thursday, go for a walk for between 25 and 40 minutes.
5. It is already Friday; relax.
6. Saturday. Walk 35-60 minutes.
7. Sunday.

   Rest.

Couch to 5k is short for "from the couch to the five-kilometer run" (C25K)

Josh Clark devised a running program called Couch to 5k, which is commonly known as C25k. It is a 9-week program based on the idea that jogging or running does not have to be monotonous. It begins with a gentle introduction to running and gradually increases the intensity weekly. Building your strength and stamina to the point where you can run a distance of 5 kilometers nonstop is the program's goal.

Set aside time for three sessions each week, and proceed according to this schedule:

1. Week One.

Begin with a walk of five minutes. The next step is to alternate between walking for 90 seconds and jogging for one minute. Maintain this interval for the next twenty minutes. That should be done for each of the sessions in the first week.

2. Week Two.

Begin with a stroll of five minutes. The next step is to alternate between running for 90 seconds and walking for 2 minutes. Maintain this interval for the next twenty minutes. It is essential to keep doing this during the second week's sessions.

3. Week Three.

Walk for the standard amount of time, which is five minutes. After then, two intervals alternate with one another. First, run for 90 seconds, then walk for 90 seconds. Repeat this three times. After that, walk for three minutes and then run for three minutes. This interval will be repeated twice more. Maintain this schedule throughout week 3 for each of the three sessions that are scheduled.

4. Week Four.

The fourth week of training is when things start to get interesting. For every session throughout the fourth week, go for a walk for five minutes.

- Run for 3 minutes.

  Walk for the next minute and a half.

- Run for 5 minutes.

  Walk for a total of two minutes and thirty seconds.

- Run for 4 minutes.

  Walk for the next minute and a half.

- Run for 5 minutes.

5. Week Five.

During the three running sessions scheduled for you during week 5, a new obstacle will be put before you to overcome.

- Variation 1 (first session this week).

The first five minutes you will spend walking, and the remaining five will be spent running. So first, you'll walk for three minutes and then run for five minutes straight. Then, continue walking for the next three minutes and start running for the last five minutes of the session.

- Variation 2 (second session this week).

The first five minutes will be spent walking, while the next eight minutes will be spent running. So first, walk for five minutes, then run for eight minutes to finish the run.

- Variation 3 (third session this week).

Walk for the first five minutes, then start running for the next 20.

6. Week Six.

In week 6, you'll have to start putting your stamina to the test! In addition, each day this week will include a unique twist on the previous one. The first variation begins with a five-minute walk, followed by five minutes of running. First, walk for three minutes, then start running for eight minutes. Walk for an additional three minutes, then end with a run for five minutes.

Option 2: After walking for the first five minutes, transition into a brisk 10-minute run.

After walking for three minutes, continue running for the remaining ten minutes to finish the run.

Option 3. Start with a five-minute walk, and then run for the next quarter of an hour.

Week seven begin each of your three workouts with the standard five-minute walk and then run nonstop for the next quarter of an hour.

8. Week Eight.

You are getting into the habit of running for longer and longer stretches! In the eighth week of your training, begin each session with a five-minute walk and end it with a 28-minute run.

9. Week Nine.

When you get to week 9, take some time to reflect on how far you've come. Walk for five minutes to begin each of the three sessions, then run for thirty minutes to wind things up.

It's normal to experience trepidation while beginning a new routine, like running. Our bodies may require some time to get used to this unique workout. Start cautiously and take it easy on yourself if you feel yourself growing fatigued or stressed. Start each of your runs at a pace that is significantly slower than the one you believe you are capable of maintaining for the whole of the run. By doing so, you will help your body improve its endurance, which will allow you to run for greater distances.

RENAULT
529

CHAPTER 4

Practical Tips to Improve Running Form

If you want to run faster, more efficiently, and more comfortably, with less stress on your body and a lower chance of injury, working on improving your running form can help. Running with the correct form lowers the likelihood of becoming fatigued and ensures that you make the most of your workout time.

If you want to work on correcting your form, follow these guidelines.

1. Look Ahead

Avoid looking down at your feet. Your gaze should be directed toward the ground around 10 to 20 feet in front of you. This is not only the correct way to run, but it is also a safer way to run because it allows you to see what is coming up ahead of you and prevents you from falling. When you run, does your head stick out in front of you? This significantly strains the neck and shoulders muscles, which can eventually lead to tension.

When you run, hold your head up so that the tops of your ears are directly over your shoulders. This will prevent your head from jutting forward as you continue the race. While running, picture yourself as a puppet pulled along by a string; keep your entire body as long and straight as possible.

2. Keep Your Hands at Your Waist at all Times.

You should try to keep your hands at waist level or just below the point where they might softly brush your hip. It is recommended that your elbows be positioned so that they form a 90-degree angle with your sides. Especially when they're exhausted, some beginners have a habit of holding their hands extremely high by their chests.

If you continue to hold your arms in that manner, you will likely become even more fatigued and begin to experience tightness and tension in your shoulders and neck. (If, on the other hand, when you are running, your arms will naturally propel your hands further back and upward.)

3. Relax Your Hands

While you're running, try to keep as little tension as possible in your arms and hands. Make sure you don't clench your hands into fists. If you tighten your fists, the strain will go up to your arms to your shoulders and neck, making you feel worse overall. You can expect this to continue as long as you maintain a tight grasp on your hands.

It's best to have a relaxed fist: Suppose that you are carrying an egg in each hand and attempting to keep it from breaking by covering it with your hands.

4. Assess Your Posture

Maintain an upright and straight posture at all times. Your shoulders should be level, your back should be straight, and your head should be up. Maintain a neutral pelvis and keep your shoulders down and under your ears. Be careful not to hunch forward or backward at the waist, as this is a typical posture for runners to adopt when they become exhausted.

Make sure to monitor your posture every once in a while. At the end of a run, when you're exhausted, it's common to slump over a little bit, which can lead to soreness in the neck, shoulders, and lower back. If you do this, you're setting yourself up for potential injury. Pull your chest out whenever you become aware that you are slouching. Keeping up a decent form near the end of your run is essential to stave off exhaustion and cross the finish line firmly.

5. Let Your Shoulders Relax

It would help if you weren't hunching your shoulders; instead, they should be relaxed and square (facing ahead). If you round your shoulders too far forward, this might cause your chest to constrict, which can make it difficult to breathe. Relaxing your shoulders will make it much simpler to take deep breaths.

Make sure your shoulders are not drawn up toward your ears and relaxed. If this is the case, bring your shoulder blades together on your back and squeeze them together as though they were elevator doors that needed to be shut. Hold them there, and let your shoulders relax down and back while you do so.

Make it a routine to check the position of your shoulders frequently to ensure that they stay relaxed in this position. Repeat the shoulder-blade squeeze motion each time you become aware that you are shrugging again.

6. Always remember to keep your arms by your sides.

Steer clear of swaying your arms from side to side. Slouching reduces the amount of oxygen taken in by your lungs with each breath because crossing your arms across your chest makes you more likely to adopt a posture that encourages slouching. Breathing that is inefficient or shallow can also cause you to get side stitches or cramps in the stomach region.

When runners become tired or tight, their hands tend to creep up towards their shoulders, which decreases the distance that separates the upper arm and the forearm. If you become aware of this, let your arms fall naturally to your sides and shake them out. Adjust your shoulders so that they are back and relaxed, then reposition them so that they are at a right angle.

7. Turn Your Arms Outwards From Your Shoulders.

Instead of moving back and forth from your elbow joint, your arms should be moving back and forth from your shoulder joint. Imagine that your arm is a pendulum suspended from your shoulder and swinging back and forth. Move your elbow backward, and then allow it to come around to face you.

When you bring your arm around to the front of your body, your hand should come very close to making contact with your hip. This is the correct position.

Your arms should be at your sides in a swinging motion. If they are going across your chest, they will start creeping up toward your shoulders, which will cause you to lean over because of the pressure they are putting on you. When you hunch your shoulders, it cannot be easy to breathe. Maintain a neutral posture by keeping your arms at your sides and parallel.

Imagine that there is a line running vertically down the middle of your body; your hands must not travel beyond that line.

8. Don't Bounce Around

When you run with too much vertical oscillation, also known as bouncing, your head and body move up and down excessively, which is inefficient and wastes a lot of energy. If you lift yourself off the ground higher, you will have to absorb a tremendous shock when you land, which will cause your legs to tire out more quickly.

Run lightly and land gently on your feet to reduce the bounce you experience and conserve energy. It would be beneficial if you tried to keep your stride low to the ground, and you should focus on having a quick stride changeover to improve your performance. Take quick, light steps as if you were walking on burning coals. Imagine who you are.

Some authorities believe that the most effective runners have a cadence of 90, meaning that their left foot strikes the ground 90 times every minute. This is also known as the turnover rate. Your cadence will increase if you walk or run with shorter steps.

Make little adjustments to your cadence and foot strike, and only practice them for brief durations. They will initially seem unnatural, and you don't want to force things too much because of this. As they become second nature to you, you will be able to perform them for longer and longer periods during your running routine.

Improve Your Form to Lower Your Risk of Injury

Gait analysis is something you should consider doing if you still have issues that can be attributed to poor running form. The Z angle, also known as the angle formed by the connection between a runner's hip and ankle, is typically evaluated by a physical therapist before a race.

How to Locate Your Z-Angle

Make use of a still shot taken of you while you were running, with the photo taken from the side while your rear foot was still on the ground. Taking a still photograph or a screenshot from a video is the most effective method for obtaining this kind of image.

Create a line across the hip joint and perpendicular to the top of your pelvis.

Make another line going down the leg you are standing on, this time from your hip to your ankle.

One final line should be drawn that goes from the joint in your ankle through each of your toes.

If you are running in the correct form, the final diagram should be in the shape of a Z.

What to Do About Improper Form

If your analysis reveals that you have problems with your form, you need to take the necessary steps to fix your technique so that you don't end up straining yourself or being injured.

If the angle is more significant at your ankle than at your hip, this may indicate either a lack of flexibility or stiffness in your calf muscles. Stretching the calves with a towel or working on strengthening the anterior tibialis muscle are two examples of exercises that may be helpful in this regard.

If the angle at your hip is greater than the angle at your ankle, this may be a sign that your hip extension is inadequate. You may find that correcting your running form with exercises like strengthening the hips or stretching the hip flexors is helpful.

Inquire With Your Primary Care Provider or Your PT

It is time to seek the counsel of your primary care physician or a physical therapist if you still have pain that you believe may be related to how you run. They will be able to evaluate your pain, examine you for any potential injuries, and give suggestions for any adjustments or exercises that might be beneficial.

On a Treadmill

If you want to lessen the effect that running has on your joints and protect yourself from overuse issues, one alternative is to run on a treadmill. During a treadmill workout, you are not compelled to slow down or stop for any reason, allowing you to maintain a speed that is both comfortable and steady. Because of this, you can concentrate entirely on your form.

Consider some of these hints and tips:

While slightly bending forward, draw your shoulders back and engage your core to strengthen your position.

Keep your back straight at all times.

Always maintain a straight line from your shoulders to your hips.

If you have balance difficulties, you should avoid holding onto the rails when running.

Put your arms at your sides, look forward, and stay away from the monitor or look down at your hands.

Take brief steps and keep your stride relatively short.

When running on a treadmill, you will need to shorten your stride in order to avoid kicking the front of the machine. If you over-stride, this will cause you to kick the front of the treadmill. This will drive you to run more efficiently.

Tips to Avoid Injuries

As you continue to focus on improving your technique, here are a few more ideas to help you avoid injury:

You can prevent injuries to your lower back and knees by improving the mobility and flexibility of your hips and ankles.

Your body will experience less stress if you increase the number of steps you take every minute.

Your runs should gradually increase in duration and intensity, and you should also run more frequently.

Increase both your speed and your mileage as time goes on.

Keep in mind that seeing results takes time.

If you are experiencing muscle soreness or injuries, especially recurrent or chronic, you should stop what you are doing and rest for a suitable amount of time.

If you have any injuries, you should get checked out by a physical therapist. They can treat your injury, determine the reason for it, and assist you in making the necessary adjustments to prevent it from happening again.

Talk to your primary care physician if you are starting an exercise routine, if you have any physical problems, or if you take any drugs that could potentially interfere with your running program.

Put on a pair of jogging shoes that are appropriate. Avoid shoes that have an excessive amount of padding in them. Replace your footwear regularly.

When it's Time to Consult an Expert

Personal training from a qualified fitness expert comes with a number of benefits that are worth considering. Working with a running expert for at least a few sessions can benefit runners of all levels, from running for fun to competing professionally.

A devoted professional can assist you in developing a tailored routine to attain your objectives while also helping you in establishing consistency, maintaining motivation, and being accountable for your actions. In addition, a professional runner will be on your team, cheering you on and assisting you in celebrating your victory after the race. It is especially advantageous if you are new to fitness or running or have any problems with your body, particularly in terms of alignment, body mechanics, or a previous injury.

Research completed in 2015 indicates that it is helpful to receive visual or auditory feedback to improve running stride to reduce the likelihood of sustaining an injury while running. Feedback is essential to improving your technique and can come in many forms, including looking in a mirror, viewing a film, or being given verbal signals.

A trained fitness professional can assist in the formation and maintenance of perfect form, as well as the elimination of any undesirable habits you may have established. They can assist you in increasing your endurance while lowering the likelihood of sustaining an injury. A trained fitness professional can help you stay safe during your workout by guiding you through the correct way to warm up, cool down, and avoid overexerting yourself. They can also guide you through developing a healthy eating plan and determining what foods to consume before and after a run.

The Bottom Line

If you want to take your running to the next level, one of the most significant ways to do it is to work on improving your running form. If you want the best results from your running regimen, you need to stick to it. Maintaining a mindful awareness of your posture throughout the day as you go from one activity to the next is essential. Concentrate on increasing the strength in your core to better support your running form as you go about your workouts.

10LB

CHAPTER 5

Diet and Nutrition for the Active Runner

When you begin running, your body may have additional nutritional requirements to meet the increased demand for energy that running causes. Eat a light meal or a snack that is high in carbohydrates (like bananas) anywhere from one to three hours before you go for a run. This is a decent rule of thumb. Instead, it would help to prioritize eating within the first two hours of returning home following a run to keep your energy.

What you need to know about maintaining a diet that is balanced and provides fuel for your runs is as follows:

1. You should consume a lot of carbohydrates.

Carbs have been portrayed as the enemy in diet culture; carbohydrates are your body's principal energy source. For this reason, athletes' carbohydrate consumption is increased just before a significant competition or race. Pasta, bread, and oats are the three foods that provide the most effective sources of carbs. Vegetables, legumes, and whole grains are also excellent sources of carbohydrates. Carbohydrates are the most critical fuel source for physical activity because they are broken down into glucose, the body's preferred energy source. Glucose is subsequently used by the body to supply energy. Therefore, exercise is an excellent way to burn carbohydrates.

Glycogen is a carbohydrate that may be stored in your muscles and liver. The glycogen stored in your muscles is the form that releases energy the fastest and is the most readily available. The caveat is that there is a limited amount of space available for storing, as you may be aware from participating in long runs and the later parts of marathons.

When your muscles are not adequately nourished, you will suffer muscle fatigue, have lower performance, and be at a higher risk of injury. If your muscles are not properly fueled, you will be at an increased risk of injury. With 500g of carbohydrates, you can run for 60 to 90 minutes at 55 to 75% of your maximum heart rate. The more you move, the more quickly your supplies will run out—those who exercise regularly likely notice that their glycogen levels have become slightly depleted over time.

When running longer than an hour, you should aim for 30–60g of carbohydrates per hour for the first three hours, then gradually increase that amount to 60–90g of carbohydrates per hour if you're still going after that. Runners may find that boiled potatoes with salt, noodle soup, or pizza satiate their hunger during longer runs over varied terrain. Because of this, it is essential to schedule your carbohydrate consumption around your workouts; the number of carbohydrates you require will vary depending on the frequency, length, and intensity of your activities.

On the verge of collapse

When runners try to complete strenuous workouts while fasting or in a condition of carbohydrate depletion due to insufficient fueling in the hours or even the day before the training, they risk several health complications.

When people find that they are not hungry immediately after a workout, they may not provide their bodies with the nutrition to facilitate healing. As a result, their ability to recover and adapt may be negatively impacted.

Both scenarios will negatively affect the body's natural hormonal control systems.

Suppose you do not stop to refuel and repair your body regularly. In that case, you risk experiencing long-term consequences that affect not only your running performance but also your overall health, such as a lowered immune system, a decrease in bone density, and a digestive system that is much slower than usual.

2. Consuming fats is essential if you want to keep going for a more extended period.

However, despite difficulty converting lipids to usable energy, your body uses fats as its next fuel source after carbs. Therefore, consider fats to be alternative forms of energy storage.

Saturated fats

Unsaturated fats

Dietary fats

Facts about Fats

Some kinds of fat are much more beneficial to one's health than others.

It is necessary to consume fat to facilitate the absorption of fat-soluble vitamins A, D, E, and K and to ensure enough intake of critical fatty acids, which the body cannot manufacture on its own. These nutrients are essential for recovery, the immune system's health, inflammation, and the avoidance of weariness. Therefore, your diet should include fat, but you should avoid using it as a source of rapid fuel because eating high-fat meals before a run will take you longer to digest food.

Not every type of fat is healthy, either.

Consuming excessive saturated fat can cause harmful cholesterol levels to rise, boosting the risk of developing cardiovascular disease. In addition, products derived from animals, such as meat and dairy, contain saturated fats. In addition, pies, cakes, cookies, fatty cuts of meat, sausages, and bacon are also sources of trans-fats. These dangerous fats are mainly found in hydrogenated oils and processed meats.

To increase the amount of the beneficial foods you consume, try eating more of the following:

- Fatty seafood, such as salmon and mackerel, which are high in omega-3 fatty acids
- Nuts and seeds, as well as the oils and butter that come from them
- Oils derived from sunflowers and olives
- Avocados

Trainers always recommend that runners consume more unsaturated fats rather than saturated ones.

Despite this, these fats still have a significant energy value, and consumers should ingest them with this proviso in mind.

3. Protein.

Your diet should include sufficient proteins essential to building solid muscles. In addition, running causes muscle breakdown and fatigue. Because of the positive effects of protein on the process of muscle regeneration, a runner's diet needs to contain an ample amount of protein.

Lean cuts of meat, such as chicken breasts, tofu, legumes, whole grains, and fish, are excellent protein sources.

Why Protein Counts

Proteins are frequently referred to as the body's "building blocks," for a good reason. Amino acids are the building blocks of proteins and are found in combination with proteins. Twenty different amino acids are the building blocks for everything from skin and hair to muscles, tendons, bones, and other tissues. Amino acids can be found in protein. In addition to these roles, they produce enzymes and carry nutrients throughout the body.

You can only get eight amino acids from your food since they are essential.

Complete proteins can be found in meals derived from animals, such as dairy products, meat, fish, and eggs. This is because these foods include a whole range of amino acids. Animal foods contain all of the essential amino acids.

Proteins derived from plants are a potential source of these compounds, but this supply is insufficient since plant-based proteins are missing one or more essential amino acids. As a result, they are found in incomplete forms.

Examples of these foods include vegetables, cereals, nuts, grains and legumes.

However, if these components are combined appropriately, a complete source of protein can be produced. The combination of baked beans and toast, rice and dhal, or peanut butter on a whole-grain bagel are just a few examples of tasty combos that are a complete protein.

Protein is a subject that receives a lot of attention in the health and fitness industry, with many people feeling that it is the macronutrient that is of the most significant value for active individuals. The fact that protein is a topic that receives a lot of attention lends credence to the assumption that this is the case. Runners mostly require protein as a response to activity rather than a fuel source for their bodies.

4. Electrolytes.

Electrolytes are essential for maintaining proper hydration levels and managing the water balance in our bodies. They help our bodies hold onto water, preventing us from dehydrating. We can experience fatigue, exhaustion, and heat cramps when we are dehydrated; therefore, we must use electrolytes to replenish water while we exercise.

Consider the following: bananas, sports drinks, and lime in water for their sodium, potassium, and magnesium content, respectively.

Hydration and the retention of electrolytes

Hydration is something that many people overlook, even though it is essential for running.

It has been demonstrated time and again that taking in fluids and maintaining an adequate level of hydration is essential not only during physical activity but also over extended periods of practice or competition. For example, consuming fluids during endurance running helps maintain hydration, thermoregulation, and enough plasma (blood) volume. This is in addition to the obvious benefit of keeping adequate blood volume.

There is a direct correlation between maintaining an adequate plasma volume and maintaining proper thermoregulation and improved performance. Plasma volume falls in response to an increase in core body temperature brought on by dehydration. This increases heart rate, accelerating the process through which weariness sets in.

These potentially harmful physiological changes can be caused by a fall in body weight of as little as one percent due to fluid loss. In addition, dehydration significantly impacts cognitive performance, reducing one's capacity to make sound judgments and choices.

Salt and Sweating

Most runners will sweat from 400 to 2,400 milliliters when running for an hour. However, this might vary based on factors such as age, gender, weight, the amount of intensity of training, and the temperature in the surrounding environment. The average is roughly 1,200 milliliters per hour, although this can change depending on these and other circumstances.

Most of what you lose through sweat is water, but you also get rid of electrolytes, primarily salt. The salt in sweat can range anywhere from 115 mg to more than 2,000 mg per 1,000 ml effort. So if a runner is known to be a "salty sweater," which refers to someone who consumes a lot of sodium, then that runner might sweat off more sodium than what is recommended.

Most electrolyte tablets, salt capsules, and sports drinks have between 250 and 300 milligrams of sodium per serving. In longer races, if you dilute your electrolytes into 750ml, you will need to consume approximately 2,250ml of fluid every hour to meet your salt requirements. This isn't easy from both a consumption and transportation point of view because it requires a significant amount of fluid. Therefore, maintaining a healthy sodium balance is essential not just when you are running but also when you are pre-training.

As a result, it shouldn't be surprising that a sizeable percentage of runners report having experienced the symptoms associated with inadequate salt consumption and dehydration. These symptoms include gastrointestinal distress, nausea, bloating, weariness, poor attention, and dizziness. However, the most common reason for stomach troubles during a run is an imbalance in sodium levels, not the consumption of sports nutrition gels or bars.

When someone is dehydrated and consumes glucose, the glucose concentration in their gut increases significantly. However, because blood is being diverted from the stomach and towards the working muscles, the digestive tract cannot absorb glucose as rapidly as it should, leading to stomach disturbances.

During longer races and training runs, it is recommended that runners take in 700–900 milligrams of sodium every hour. Salt tablets, electrolyte supplements, energy drinks, and even food, if you have the stomach, can be included in this combination (e.g., salted peanuts, cured meat). Maintaining a healthy sodium balance while running and before beginning training or in the days preceding competition is vital. To help runners avoid the problems described above, it is recommended that they begin consuming electrolyte-containing fluids precisely one day before the race.

5. Fiber.

It is vitaly important to restrict the amount of fiber you consume before jogging. Because fiber makes you feel full, drinking enough to give your body the nutrition it needs before indulging in strenuous physical activity, like running, may be difficult for you because it makes you feel full.

Because fiber is an essential component of any diet, it would be beneficial for you to reduce the amount of fiber you consume in the days leading up to the very strenuous activity. However, fiber should not be deleted from the diet entirely.

Having said all this, various people have different ways of digesting food. Please note the foods you consume and the times of day when you do so. Different kinds of food may have varied effects on you depending on the time of day you consume them.

Consult with a nutritionist if you want answers to any queries regarding the foods that are healthiest for your body.

Do Runners Even Need Supplements?

No is the short and straightforward response. Supplements for running are designed to do what their name suggests: they are intended to supplement your daily intake if you are not obtaining enough through the food you eat. It is not impossible at all to meet the recommended daily consumption of any dietary supplement through dietary consumption alone. However, many of us cannot consistently maintain the ideal diet because of the demands of our jobs, personal lives, stress levels, and families.

Here are some suggestions for supplements to take when running:

A Compendium of the Finest Nutritional Supplements for Runners

1. Branched Chains Amino Acids (BCAA)

When we run, we lose a significant amount of muscle mass, which is related to the fact that when we become slimmer, we lose more muscle mass. Therefore, even if you run regularly, you still have the potential to wind up with a calorie deficit. While jogging, taking BCAA's will assist you in keeping as much muscle as possible intact.

You are in a catabolic condition if you are not obtaining adequate nourishment, which is the case whether you are dieting or training for a marathon. This can happen for several reasons. As a result, you may have muscular and joint pain, fatigue, and difficulty falling asleep or staying asleep at night.

You will experience a decrease in power due to your body's usage of amino acids, which are generally committed to the process of protein synthesis, as a source of energy for developing more muscles. This is because your body breaks down fat and some muscle — basically tissue — rather than making it. This will result in you losing muscle.

My go-to supplement is Life Extension's Branch Chain Amino Acids which come in capsule form and is the one I believe to be the best for athletes.

When to take it: The muscle cells in your body receive additional energy from the amino acids in a BCAA supplement, which helps minimize symptoms of weariness and improves overall performance. BCAA's are one of the runners' most excellent post-workout supplements because they increase your muscle growth and recovery after you run.

2. Glutamine

The following is a synopsis of the advantages that glutamine, a non-essential amino acid that offers to runners who consume it:

It does this by providing sustenance to the cells that are part of your immune system, thereby helping to maintain both the volume and hydration of those cells.

Our blood plasma and muscles both contain glutamine as a natural component; however, high levels of physical stress and strenuous exercise have been shown to reduce the amount of glutamine in our plasma. When our glutamine levels get too low, we risk becoming ill if we do not restore them. Therefore, a dosage of 20 milligrams is suggested to stop the catabolic process from taking place in our muscles.

Even though glutamine is an excellent supplement for jogging, it should not be used in place of adequate amounts of rest and recovery time. This nutrient improves rehydration, endurance, muscle growth, and recovery time. It also encourages a healthy digestive system and stimulates the formation of beneficial digestive bacteria.

When to take it: I take my glutamine supplement immediately upon leaving the gym in the morning. You will notice the most improvement after a rigorous workout.

3. Probiotics

Our immune system, brain, and hormones can be affected, either positively or negatively, by the condition of our gut. Another factor that can lead to increased inflammation throughout our systems is low levels of the flora (bacteria) that live in our digestive tract. Inadequate levels of gut flora (bacteria) are another factor that might contribute to increased inflammation throughout our bodies.

Probiotic supplements can dramatically improve your digestive tract's health and boost your immune system. In addition to promoting heart health and relieving symptoms of various digestive ailments, probiotics help restore a healthy balance to the beneficial bacteria in our digestive tract. You can find it in foods such as yogurt, sauerkraut, tempeh, kimchi, miso, and kombucha, but you can also take a supplement for it as I do. When to take it: I take this dietary supplement before bed at night.

4. L-Carnitine

When bodybuilding, most people take L-carnitine to help them lose weight or gain muscle. But should runners take L-carnitine to improve their performance?

At the same time as it assists in the development of muscles, L-carnitine facilitates the breakdown of fat stored in the body to release ATP.

It is a fantastic supplement for anyone who is naturally burning fat. L-carnitine functions by moving long-chain fatty acids into the mitochondria of cells for the goal of producing energy. This makes it suitable for anyone who is interested in burning fat or gaining muscle. As a result of its ability to transfer long-chain fatty acids into the mitochondria of cells to produce energy, it is an excellent supplement for anyone who is naturally burning fat while they run.

L-carnitine is a dietary supplement that helps boost athletic performance by converting the fat stored in our bodies into ATP. In addition, this nutrient can assist our bodies in producing maximal oxygen use by increasing the number of red blood cells created.

When to take it: On an empty stomach, I consume 1500 milligrams of L-carnitine first thing in the morning.

What exactly is the term "acetyl L-carnitine"?

It is a specialized form of carnitine that can boost levels of carnitine in the brain, where it may burn fat to provide energy for brain cells. Acetyl L-carnitine is a form of carnitine that can accomplish this. This is particularly significant since cells require energy to repair any harm they have sustained to continue their existence. Additionally, it would help to consume this dietary supplement first thing in the morning.

5. Calcium

Runners should pay attention to their bone health to support their joints. Calcium consumption is an absolute necessity for humans because our bones are the source of many different types of injuries, including stress fractures, knee problems, and many more. The human skeleton serves as a storage mechanism for calcium. For it to perform its metabolic purpose, it needs a sufficient amount of calcium to prevent calcium from being drawn from bone stores. If pulling takes place, it has the potential to leave your body in an unfavorable state of calcium balance, which may ultimately result in bone loss.

I suggest going with one of the many kinds of calcium, such as calcium Citrate. It is available for purchase in any pharmacy or on iherb.com.

When to take it: I take 500 milligrams of calcium at any time of the day with meals.

6. Omega 3 Fish Oil

Runners can protect themselves from the adverse effects of inflammation by taking in the omega-3 fatty acids found in fish oil. Because humans can't make omega-3 fatty acids, the only way to get them is to consume foods rich in them or take dietary supplements that contain them. If you're a runner, there are many reasons to take advantage of fish oil, including the performance-boosting benefits, such as increasing muscle growth, improving strength, and enhancing your overall physical performance. Because of its ability to minimize exercise-induced muscle damage and delayed-onset muscle soreness, fish oil has emerged as one of the most popular dietary supplements for runners, particularly regarding recovery and endurance.

Fish oil has been a massive help for me in reducing the discomfort I have due to the negative impact that intense training has had on my immune system for a very long time. I recommend purchasing fish oil capsules from Now Foods because they are high quality and will not leave your mouth with any fishy flavor after being consumed.

When to take it: I take anywhere from one to three capsules before bed at night.

7. Vitamins C and E

Vitamins C and E are potent antioxidants that provide an incredible amount of support, particularly for runners who compete in long-distance events. Your immune system receives a boost from vitamin C, which also assists in the battle against oxidative damage, which can be produced by physical activity and environmental contaminants. In addition to that, it can mend cartilage, bones, and teeth.

On the other hand, Vitamin E helps your body battle the free radical damage caused by exercising for an extended period. Vitamin E also helps maintain your heart and the cardiovascular system as a whole.

If you do not consume adequate amounts of vitamin C, you may notice that your muscles become less potent. I've been taking this Lypospheric Vitamin C supplement, and I've found that it does a great job of helping my health. It is undoubtedly the most effective Vitamin C supplement available on the market.

To get your daily dose of vitamin E, I suggest taking this supplement in conjunction with vitamin C. This dietary supplement should be consumed before retiring for the night.

8. Magnesium

If you want to run a marathon, it would be beneficial to have a lot of endurance.

Magnesium is an essential element of our diet and can significantly impact our ability to run faster over longer distances. This mineral is an essential factor in many body activities, including the production of energy, the contraction of muscles, the maintenance of healthy bones and muscles, and the correct operation of the circulatory and nervous systems. Because it also assists in relaxing our bodies, it is frequently sold as a supplement for improving sleep quality.

When to take it: Taking it right before going to bed is essential to ensure that you get sufficient time to rest and recover.

9. Vitamin D3

Runners who experience troubles with eye twitching can benefit significantly from taking a medication that contains vitamin D3. When you're under a lot of stress, drinking inadequate amounts of water, or not getting enough sleep, this is something that frequently occurs.

If you want to preserve your bones from breaking down, running is an excellent activity to combine with taking calcium and vitamin D supplements. This combination is beneficial for runners. Runners who already struggle with osteoporosis will find this information helpful. Vitamin D3 is known to improve the quality of sleep. Thus the optimum time to take it is before going to bed.

10. Caffeine

Caffeine, on its own, without any additions of milk or sugar, is my go-to choice for ensuring that I have sufficient energy for running.

Try drinking a caffeinated beverage before a workout when looking for a supplement to help run marathons. Before starting your workout regimen at the end of a long day at work, consider relaxing with a cup of black coffee to unwind from the stress of the day. Since I'm not too fond of the taste of coffee, I drink a cup of green tea first thing in the morning. If you want coffee, consider drinking a cup in its three roasting varieties: blonde, medium, or dark roast.

Runners have particular nutritional requirements and concerns. It is necessary to fully fuel your training and recovery to feel and perform at your maximum best. Doing so will allow you to reach your full potential in both areas. A well-thought-out strategy for the day of the race can provide you with a competitive edge by ensuring sufficient energy for optimal performance and protecting you from the possibility of gastrointestinal problems.

During your training, it is vital to keep track of the meals you eat and how you feel as a result of eating those foods because the things that work for you as a runner may not be the same for other runners. After that, you will have a much clearer understanding of how the food you eat affects your body, and you will be able to make the appropriate adjustments based on that knowledge.

CHAPTER 6

Effective Strategies on How to Become a Better Runner

Developing one's running will imply a variety of things to a variety of different people. There will be some participants whose focus will be on breaking their records (PR). Others will be getting ready for their first, second, or even third marathon with their training.

For what are you putting in all this effort? What specific ways do you hope to grow as a runner? It is vital to perform an objective analysis of the situation from time to time, which requires taking a few steps back. It takes a lot of self-awareness to take a step back and recognize when you are on the verge of experiencing some discomfort or harm.

To become a better runner, you must balance pushing yourself to your limits and going beyond those boundaries. Finding this balance is the key to improving your running. Reading this chapter will help you improve as a runner while also reducing your risk of injuries and exhaustion. If you want to become a better runner, you should work on improving in the following ways:

1. Vow to yourself that you will appear every day.

Simply showing up requires you to get out the door and start running. Other times, showing up may mean listening to your body and having a leisurely or rest day. These are examples of what we mean by saying "show up." The fact that you are consistently working toward achieving your objectives and goals is what matters.

2. Running and resting are equally necessary activities.

Include days off in your routine so that your muscles have the opportunity to recuperate and grow. If you're having trouble relaxing during your rest days, try going for a swim or riding your bike. This will get your body working differently than it usually would.

3. Switch up the way you usually run.

You should become familiar with how to vary your jogging routine if you want to take your running to the next level.

- Long runs.

When you're doing a lengthy run, you want to spend as much time as possible on your legs. These next few days will develop your endurance. When you need a break throughout a lengthy run, slow down to a jog or walk for a few minutes before continuing.

- Interval runs.

Interval runs consist of bursts of high-energy running broken up by periods of lower-intensity running. To properly perform interval training, you need to sprint at predetermined intervals and alternate those sprints with periods of jogging or walking. Start running again as soon as your heart rate returns to normal. Your speed can be improved by interval training.

- Tempo runs.

Tempo runs are runs in which you teach your body to run at a pace that is faster than your goal pace for a more extended amount of time. For example, in re-runs, you train your body to run at your goal pace for an extended period. You do this by running at your goal pace.

Before beginning your tempo runs, complete an easy warm-up run that lasts between 5 and 15 minutes. After that, keep your pace consistent for an extended period while you run at your goal speed. As the last step, you should finish each jog at a slower pace as a cool-down.

4. Include some form of strength training.

Exercises that build strength allow your muscles to grow larger and strengthen your bones. You may improve your running in all aspects—strength, endurance, and speed—by including strength training as part of your weekly running program. Strength exercises are any physical activity in which you use resistance, such as lifting weights or performing pushups.

5. Include training in maintaining your equilibrium.

Balancing exercises can enhance your balance, which will assist in preventing falls when you are running on different terrains, such as when you are jogging on the trails or going for a long run.

6. When establishing your running goals, make sure you are both realistic and ambitious.

Learn to strike a balance between being ambitious and being overambitious as you work toward achieving your running objectives. Ask yourself if you have sufficient time to train towards your goal reasonably. If you feel that you are putting yourself in danger of getting hurt, you should reevaluate the goals you have set for yourself.

When it comes to working toward your running objectives, how far are you willing to push yourself? Will it be challenging to give yourself time off to relax and recharge? After the day, you ought to ask yourself: does how I've performed today correspond to the amount of preparation I've put in? If you find that a particular run is enjoyable, there is a good chance that you will want to repeat it. However, studies have shown that switching up your regimen and exercising different muscles at varying intensities is essential. That way will bring you a more significant number of benefits.

Modifying the most minor aspects of your running technique, such as your posture or footwear, can significantly impact your performance.

You can quickly advance from being a beginner runner to an experienced one by implementing a few strategies outlined here.

Get started slowly.

According to Melissa Merritt, a personal trainer based in Los Angeles, if you have never run before or if it has been a while, you shouldn't expect to run five miles on day one, especially if you haven't run in a long time.

Instead, she suggested creating a timetable and sticking to it gradually to ease into the activity. According to Merritt's explanation, "Being consistent will help you build up your endurance and ensure that you're setting yourself up for success." Merritt encourages her customers to be kind to themselves and to look past the challenging days in their lives.

She offered this piece of advice, "Small steps can add up," and pointed out that "some days will be fantastic and others might suck, but as long as you have more nice days and overall appreciate the process, persist with it, and it will get easier." She went on to say that "Small steps can add up."

7. Identify a specific objective to work towards.

Former "Biggest Loser" trainer Jillian Michaels suggests that signing up for an upcoming race at the beginner level is one of the most effective strategies to accelerate one's progress in the sport of running. She advised, "Pick a cause that's essential to you, whether it's raising money to combat breast cancer or AIDS." "Be sure to set a date and a crystal clear target. Make sure people know you are participating, emotionally prepare yourself, register for the event, and collect donations.

Michaels, who has only recently released a running training program for beginners on her app, pointed out that it is reasonable for a runner who has never run before to be ready for a 5,000-meter race in just two months. Joining a running group is recommended as "another method to keep yourself accountable and to empower yourself with emotional support," she explained.

8. Get your head in the game and get ready to run.

It was pointed out by Joan Scrivanich, a running and triathlon coach with rising endurance, that mental training can significantly increase your performance when you are pavement-pounding. When Henry Ford famously stated, "Whether you think you can, or you think you can't, you're right," he was correct.

According to what Scrivanich asserted, the mind and the body are inextricably linked, and better confidence levels are directly correlated to improved performance. This mindset explains why athletes frequently perform better after picturing a task, such as weightlifting, before attempting to accomplish the action itself.

9. Put some effort into your strength training.

According to Rachel Straub, a co-author of the book Weight Training Without Injury, to excel in running and prevent injuries, it is essential to keep your body as strong as possible. According to Straub, one of the most important things a runner can do to improve their performance is to ensure that they include strength training activities as part of their regular regimen.

The knee is the body part that suffers the most damage from runners' injuries, and the main contributor is a lack of hip strength. Straub states, "when your hips are weak, this increases loading at the knee." Exercises such as side steps with a resistance band, bridges, squats, and hip extensions were some of the training activities she suggested.

"Even if you don't have a gym membership, you can still practice pointing and flexing your foot by connecting a band around the leg of your sofa. According to Michaels, you can do the exercise by wrapping the band to the top of the foot and pulling it forward. "A simple hold in which you draw your toes back and compress the front of your shins is equally efficient." It's also possible to employ a quick hold in which you bring your toes toward the back of your shins and pressure the front of your shins.

10. Always maintain your flexibility.

Following a run, Michaels is a strong advocate for stretching in the correct manner. To conduct calf stretches, the fitness instructor recommends either letting your heel dangle off of a step or using a wall to drive your toes backward in order to feel the stretch in your calf. Both of these methods are effective.

Karena Wu, who owns Active Care Physical Therapy locations in both New York and Mumbai, recommended that runners take the time to perform some static stretches. These stretches help promote flexibility, which is beneficial for long distance running, and they also aid to slow down the pulse rate. Because it can assist in the movement of lactic acid out of the muscular tissues, this results in decreased muscle tightness and soreness after exercise, as discovered by Wu.

11. Run Through the Hills

Hill runs are the most basic kind of speed-work session since it's simple to plan them out, they don't need much thought, and even if they hurt a lot, they're over within a hurry. "Uphill training is wonderful for the glutes; keep your heart rate up, and stress your body's capability to metabolize lactic acid," adds elite runner and coach Shaun Dixon. "Boosting your speed is one of the most important factors in improving your speed."

"Locate a hill with a severe incline, sprint up it for thirty to forty-five seconds, then stroll down it. Do this six to ten times." You might also choose to run down the slope instead.

Dixon states, "Kenyan runners frequently engage in downhill sessions to enhance their foot turnover." This method keeps your feet moving quickly to avoid the severe jarring in your joints.

"Look for a hill that has a moderate slope.

Once you've reached the peak, take a deep breath and stand tall; lean forward slightly as you begin your descent. Concentrate on quickly bringing up your heels and taking short, quick steps while also focusing on creating soft, light, and immediate contact with the ground. You can try anywhere from six to ten repetitions of thirty seconds spent running downhill, following each repetition with a jog to the top of the hill.

12. Consider Joining a Club

Running by yourself can be one of life's greatest joys, but running with other people can help you stay motivated, meet new friends, and learn about new areas to go when you're following a training program that requires you to complete multiple runs per week.

You'll be able to locate free running groups in most cities across the UK now; in fact, many stores that specialize in running put on numerous group runs each week. Alternatively, you can investigate the possibility of joining your community's running club.

You may relax knowing that you do not need to be a speed demon to join because they accommodate people of all different abilities.

13. Get Gait Analysis

Gait analysis is a service that is provided for free at several specialized running retailers.

You will be videotaped while running on a treadmill for a couple of minutes, and the footage will then be played back (in freeze-frame if necessary) to evaluate your foot plant, stride, and running pattern. This information is then utilized to choose the shoe best suited for your needs; however, it is essential to note that you should not place more importance on the results of your gait analysis than on what your feet are trying to tell you.

If you try out a pair of shoes and find that you enjoy how they feel when you wear them, then you should buy them. This is the rule that you should follow most of the time.

14. Please Don't Wear Out Your Shoes.

Your running shoes will significantly impact various terrains and in all kinds of weather, so you should plan on replacing them regularly. Generally, it would help if you replaced a pair of tires every 500 to 600 miles (800-960km). If you try to get a few more weeks of use out of worn shoes, they will not provide you with the necessary protection, and you will increase your risk of getting injured. The frequency with which you buy new shoes will vary depending on your weight, running style, and choice of terrain. However, it would help if you never tried to stretch the life of shoes worn out for any time.

15. Choose some higher-tech socks.

When you get your shoes fitted, you should always wear the socks you plan to use for running in them. Significantly when your feet expand due to the heat, the thickness of your socks can dramatically impact how your shoes fit and feel on your feet.

Socks designed specifically for running offer additional cushioning in the ball of the foot, the toes, and the area around the heel. Runners should always wear socks designed for running. The additional padding absorbs more of the force of the contact and protects vital areas prone to blistering. In addition, there is typically padding or a more constricted space through the arch, which enables the shoe to fit more closely and adds more arch support.

16. Complete Your Athletic Attire Collection

When you've got your running shoes and socks figured out, it's time to turn your attention to the rest of your equipment. T-shirts and shorts are typically the mainstays of any runner's wardrobe, and you should prioritize having running gear that is lightweight, breathable, and wicks away sweat. After that, it is all about the weather you will be exposed to.

A running jacket that shields you from the wind and rain is an investment that will pay off if you plan to exercise outside during the winter months. Additionally, base layers and running tights are essential partners in the battle against the cold.

After running for a while, you'll almost certainly start thinking about how you can become a better and faster runner. When you start running, your goals will probably be straightforward and not focused on speed, such as getting fitter or spending more time outside. However, after some time, you'll almost certainly start thinking about how you can become a better and faster runner.

These suggestions will be helpful.

17. Get Stronger

"If you want to be faster, first work on getting stronger," advises Dixon. "Work on developing strength and mobility of your hips, knees, and ankles, as well as improving your overall flexibility." In addition, work on increasing strength in your glutes, legs, and core. If you begin to think like an athlete, you will eventually start to perform like one.

18. Take it Easy and Don't Overdo It

According to Justin Craig, co-owner of the running specialty store RUN Detroit in Michigan, "there's no rhyme or reason to the fact that some days are just hard." The essential thing is to keep moving forward, but you should also be aware of your body and try to avoid pushing yourself further than you can.

Craig gave the following advice: "Do everything you can to adapt." The instructor remarked that this might necessitate slowing down or cutting a run short. It would help if you avoided the mindset of "win at any cost"; instead, pay heed to what your body is trying to tell you. You're begging to get injured if you put too much pressure on yourself before you're ready for it.

The Most Important Tip for New Runners

The most critical tip to becoming a runner is to get started. So lace up your shoes and (following our warm-up advice) get out there! Whether you want to become a marathoner or complete a Couch to 5k program, all it takes is action and intelligent training.

CHAPTER 7

Helpful Strategies for Runners Who Want to Shed Some Pounds

Jotting down everything you consume for a few weeks in a journal might be a valuable tool to fight against mindless or excessive eating. Reviewing a record of your food consumption will assist you in determining the areas of your diet that need modification. Additionally, because you are aware that you will need to record it later, it may force you to reconsider eating that chocolate-covered donut, which will assist you in maintaining your current course of action. Finally, it's common for runners to report that they are perpetually hungry, so you'll want to try to organize your meals and snacks so that you don't overeat.

The following are some more suggestions that can help you keep your diet on track:

- Consume meals that are more moderate in size:

Instead of eating three large meals, try spreading your caloric intake across five or six smaller meals. This can assist in keeping your metabolism and energy levels stable and minimize hunger sensations, leading to unhealthy behaviors like overeating.

- Be mindful of the calories you consume from liquids. Even if you may be jogging a lot, you do not need to refuel your body with energy drinks and sports drinks continuously. The same is true for coffee, fruit juices, and soda beverages. Simply drinking water is sufficient to meet your needs in this regard.

- Reduce the number of carbs you eat. The average adult should consume between 225 and 325 grams of carbohydrates daily on a diet of 2,000 calories. This equates to around 45–65 percent of the total daily calorie intake. If you are above or within this range but still cannot lose weight, you should substitute some carbs with lean protein and limit your carbohydrate intake.

Running for Exercise

A large number of calories can be burned in a short amount of time through the activity of running. When you run, the number of calories you burn will differ depending on factors such as your body size, how fast you run, and how long you run. However, as a comprehensive rule of thumb, many runners of average stature estimate that they burn approximately 100 calories per mile when they run.

A study that the National Weight Control Registry carried out found that those who successfully lost weight and maintained their new weight for an extended period burned roughly 2,800 calories per week through exercise. To burn an average of 100 calories each mile, you must run approximately 28 miles a week. This means that jogging alone can help you lose weight if it's the only exercise you undertake.

Don't stress how fast you're going or how hard you're working out; concentrate on building up your mileage while maintaining a regular weekly plan. You should prepare for your runs ahead and schedule them like any other significant event. Running will, at some point, help you burn the calories necessary to achieve your weight loss goals.

Running Workouts

Depending on the types of running workouts, it could take longer or shorter to achieve the weight loss objectives you have set for yourself. Even while there is no "perfect" running routine to lose weight, it is possible to increase the weight loss you achieve by combining different forms of exercise.

Burning Carbs vs. Burning Fat

When you exercise, the ratio of carbohydrates to fat that your body needs for fuel might alter depending on the speed of the workout, how long it lasts, and how intense it is.

Take into consideration the following:

- Running at a high intensity causes the body to rely more on carbohydrates simply because they are a source of energy released more quickly. When you begin an activity that requires a burst of energy, such as sprinting, they give your body the boost of energy that it needs. It's the same as setting a match to paper; the fire burns hotter and faster at first, but it goes out just as quickly.

- Runs with a lower intensity: When you do runs that are longer but have lower power, your body gradually changes its fuel source from carbohydrates to fat. Even though fats may not be used quickly as a source of fuel, they are a more sustainable option.

Burning fat is comparable to lighting a candle because it maintains its flame for extended periods. If you would like to reduce the amount of fat stored in your body, you should perform your workouts at a slower but more consistent pace throughout the entire session. This makes the most sense if your goal is to reduce the amount of fat stored in your body. Although working out at a lower level will enable you to burn more calories from fat, working out at a higher intensity will result in a more significant number of calories being burned overall.

Workouts That Help You Burn More Calories

When you run at a faster speed, you will expend more calories because you will be working at a level of intensity closer to 80 or 90 percent of your maximum heart rate. At this rate, you are not running at full speed but working so hard that you cannot carry on a conversation. So, to begin, complete a 20-minute run at an intensity level between 80 and 90 percent.

Interval training is another option in which you switch between high-intensity and low-intensity bouts of exercise at regular intervals.

You should be able to extend the time of the intervals and the number of repetitions as you progress and become more physically fit. It would help if you didn't always run at such a quick pace. After engaging in any physically demanding activity, you need to provide your body with the opportunity to recuperate and rebuild itself.

It is not unreasonable to perform one or two runs of vigorous-intensity each week. On the remaining days of the week, you should accomplish lengthier runs that are less strenuous. These runs will seem more manageable, allowing you to log longer kilometers and burn a more significant number of calories than before. As a final suggestion, if you want to break up your monotony while increasing your strength, try running up and down hills or on an indoor treadmill.

Workouts that build muscle

Your running training should include significant time spent doing nothing but walking. Strength training should be incorporated into a runner's regular regimen if they wish to experience weight loss sustained over time. Increasing your lean muscle mass during strength training will help you burn calories and boost your running performance, thanks to the increased muscle mass. When you run, you'll be able to run for greater distances, quicker for more extended periods, and burn more calories overall. Even when you're not doing anything, having a healthy lean muscle mass might help you burn more calories throughout the day.

Strength training helps avoid running injuries, which means that you'll be able to keep up with your commitment to exercise even if you don't have to miss any workouts due to a nagging injury. Try completing at least one resistance training session or weight lifting weekly. Make sure that your weekly workout plan includes time for two to three sessions of twenty to thirty minutes each dedicated to strength training. Of course, lifting huge weights is not required to make a difference in the world. However, exercises using only one's body weight can be pretty practical.

The Most Frequent Concerns and Errors

When you run to lose weight, you must ensure that your goals are realistic. If you've been trying to lose weight but haven't seen the results you were hoping for, there may be a valid explanation for why. Think about some of these questions that runners frequently ask and some of the typical myths that could lead to confusion.

Should I eat after every run?

Refueling after a run is essential, but how you do so is very crucial if your objective is to lose weight. Your hunger will grow simply from exercising because your body will require more calories to keep itself functioning normally. If you are not careful and consume an excessive amount of improper foods, you risk surpassing the energy your body needs.

According to several studies, the period following exercise in which muscle glycogen stores are most responsive to rebuilding is thirty minutes. Therefore, it's been hypothesized that if you eat quickly after a strenuous workout or long run, you can reduce the amount of muscular soreness you experience. After your run, choose food with manageable serving sizes, such as a post-run smoothie, a glass of chocolate milk, a banana, or a cup of yogurt. When planning your meals, prioritize foods high in fiber and protein so that you can eat less but still feel content.

Why don't I seem to be able to lose weight?

A weight-loss rate of between one and two pounds per week is considered healthy and appropriate. If you are routinely running and doing strength training, you may lose weight, but more likely, you are growing muscle simultaneously. If this is your situation, the end effect is that your body is becoming fitter, stronger, and leaner, despite the possibility that the scale will suggest a difference. There are situations where you can even experience an increase in weight.

Think about switching up the way you keep track of your accomplishments.

Either take your measurements or pay attention to how differently the garments you wear fit might help you calculate your percentage of body fat.

Should I go without food?

When you are fasting, there are fewer carbohydrates in your system, and your body can more efficiently burn fat. As a result, fasting can help you lose weight. When you are not fasting, however, there are carbohydrates in your system. In the state known as "fasting," a person abstains from eating any food. On the other hand, this does not suggest that you participate in physical activity while you are hungry.

According to some research, working out on an empty stomach may result in workout sessions that are both shorter and less effective. So instead, it would help if you began your morning with a snack that ranges from 100 to 200 calories and is rich in protein and carbohydrates. This will provide you with sufficient nutrition for your workout and may even help to reduce your appetite once you have done your training.

If I cut back on my workouts, would I still see results?

When it comes to losing weight successfully, consistency is the most critical factor in any program, especially running. Running is a physically demanding activity.

It's possible that running every day, or even once every other day, is too strenuous for some people. However, you won't receive the benefits of exercise if you do it only on an infrequent basis. It would help if you tried incorporating other training forms into your running routines, such as weightlifting, rowing, cycling, or trekking. This will help you stay in shape and improve your running performance. Make it a goal to engage in some form of physical activity on most days of the week.

Individuals who engage in 250 to 300 minutes of moderate physical activity each week lose the most weight the fastest, according to study conducted by the American College of Sports Medicine.

Does it make a difference what time of day it is?

The question of when in the day one should engage in the most physical activity is hotly contested. However, the research indicates that the advantages of exercise are at their peak when the participant's core temperature is at its maximum point. This occurs for people between 4 and 5 p.m., while some studies extend this time to 7 p.m.

However, the time of day when you are most inspired to exercise is the best indicator of when you should schedule your workouts. Therefore, make sure you plan your runs during a time of day when you are confident you will be able to complete them.

Most fitness professionals suggest running first thing in the morning because other commitments are less likely to interfere with your workout if you wake up earlier. However, early workouts aren't always the best option for people. If you aren't sure, try out a few various schedules to discover which one works best for you and experiment with that one.

The Most Effective Part of the Day to Work Out

Will running help reduce the fat around my stomach area? Running will not result in spot reduction of body fat (or any specific kind of exercise). Instead, some runners' primary focus should be reducing the amount of belly fat they carry. Even though many people are concerned about how extra fat in the abdominal region looks, there are legitimate reasons to be concerned about fat in this region of the body from a health perspective.

You don't just have fat underneath your skin; there's also fat deep inside your body, all-around your essential organs, if you have abdominal fat. Visceral fat is a specific kind of fat, and the more of it a person has, the greater their chance of developing severe health diseases such as type 2 diabetes, heart disease, hypertension, high cholesterol, and breathing problems.

For women, having a waist circumference less than 35 inches is associated with a lower risk of severe health problems. In addition, visceral fat is associated with these health issues. For men, the desired waist size is under 40 inches.

Even if you don't adjust your diet, the good news is that research has shown that moderate to high-intensity aerobic activity, like jogging, can help reduce visceral fat in the body.

However, the most effective method for overall weight loss and visceral fat loss is combining aerobic exercise with a healthy diet low in calories. Although activity appears to be more effective than diet in targeting visceral fat, combining the two methods is the most effective.

Additional Weight Loss Advice from the Experts

Listed below are various approaches to weight loss that emphasize the need to combine a regular jogging program with a diet rich in nutritious foods but low in calories.

- Make some simple adjustments to your diet:

Concentrate on making modest adjustments to your diet, such as eliminating regular soda and increasing the number of fresh fruits and vegetables in your meals.

- Try to stay away from processed foods:

It is sometimes tough to lose weight since the ingredients in packaged goods and snack meals are filled with trans-fats, added sugar, and added salt. These three things can all make it more difficult to shed unwanted pounds.

- Practice portion control:

Be mindful of the portions you consume, especially after running, when you might be tempted to eat a bit more than usual because of the number of calories you burned off during your run. Put together some well-balanced 100-calorie snacks ahead of time and keep them in the house. Then, you won't be able to give in to the temptation to overindulge, and you'll be able to rest assured that you'll always have access to selections that are beneficial to your health. When dining out, split your meal with a companion or eat half and take the other half with you.

- Make sure to check the labels on food:

Food that is low in fat does not necessarily mean that it is also low in carbohydrates and sugar. Sugar is sometimes added to dishes to compensate for the flavor lost when fat is reduced. It's common for foods like salad dressings, marinades, mayonnaise, and sauces to conceal significant amounts of fat and a lot of calories.

- Strive for satisfaction:

  Instead of eating until you are full, focus on becoming aware of the point at which you feel satisfied. Because of this, you won't consume extra calories that aren't required.

- Slow down:

You may eat more slowly and enjoy what you're eating if you concentrate on the meal in front of you and take the time to experience the flavor and texture of each bite. To achieve satiety more rapidly and with less effort, try cutting your food into more manageable bits and chewing each one thoroughly.

- Eliminate all of the interruptions:

When you eat while watching television or trying to perform multiple tasks at once, you will likely consume more food than you intended to because you will not be paying attention to what you are doing. Therefore, make it a priority to restrict your eating to times and places where you can maintain complete awareness of the kind and amount of food you put into your mouth at any given moment.

Running is a beautiful exercise that can help you achieve your weight loss goals and burn calories. By burning calories more efficiently, it helps you reduce weight as well as build muscle and endurance.

If you want to lose weight and improve your level of fitness at the same time, you should combine a regular plan of jogging with strength training and a healthy diet. After that, you should engage in running to prevent the weight from creeping back in.

It has a higher caloric expenditure than the majority of exercises.

Many distinct muscles must work hard together for running to burn calories faster than most other forms of exercise (Trusted Source). High-intensity interval training (HIIT) burns the most calories per minute by utilizing a wide range of muscles at their utmost potential.

Research shows that running burns more calories than other forms of exercise.

Running a mile (1,600 meters) on either a treadmill or a track burns more calories than a research study involving 12 men and 12 women found. Running on the treadmill burns 33 more calories than walking, while running a mile on the track burns 35 more calories than walking on average (3Trusted Source). At first glance, a person running burns around 330–350 more calories per mile than walking throughout the length of a 10-mile walk.

Over 30 minutes, Harvard University researchers compared the number of calories burnt by participants of three different weights. They found that running at a moderate six mph pace burned 372 calories in 30 minutes for a 155-pound (70-kg) person (10 km per hour). This burns as many calories as swimming, martial arts, and even more than a 30-minute basketball match.

Running at a High Intensity after Exercise Continues to Burn Calories

Only jogging, swimming, and biking will continue to burn calories after you finish your workout.

However, hill runs or interval training can keep your metabolism working for 48 hours after you finish your workout (5Trusted Source). These workouts use many muscles and require additional energy to recover afterward. It's called the "afterburn effect" among fitness enthusiasts. The "afterburn effect," according to some research, may help you burn more calories over time (6Trusted Source, 7Trusted Source).

Ten men cycled for 45 minutes at an intensive speed to determine how many calories they burnt after the workout and for how long. Over 14 hours following the training, the typical participant expended an additional 190 calories (7Trusted Source). The "afterburn effect" can also be seen in high-intensity running, even though the example used cycling. Again, this is because cyclists are a convenient method of calculating calories burned in a controlled laboratory experiment.

Running at a high intensity suppresses hunger and encourages you to eat less. Eating less or modifying the food you consume is a standard method of decreasing one's caloric consumption. Unfortunately, these methods may sometimes merely boost appetite, making it more difficult to shed extra pounds. However, high-intensity running has been shown to reduce your hunger after a workout, which may help you lose weight. Several studies have discovered this (8Trusted Source, 9Trusted Source).

High-intensity running may reduce hunger by reducing the levels of the hunger hormone ghrelin and increasing the production of satiety hormones such as peptide YY. However, the precise mechanisms underlying this response are unknown. Ghrelin levels in males were dropped by 60 minutes of running or 90 minutes of weight training, according to a study involving 11 men. PYY production has increased solely due to running (8Trusted Source).

Another experiment, including nine males, examined the impact on ghrelin production of 60 minutes of running versus no exercise, and compared to no training, running decreased ghrelin levels for three to nine hours (9Trusted Source).

Running can help you lose weight because it burns a lot of calories. In addition to burning many calories during the workout, it also helps you continue to burn calories after you stop working.

Running also provides numerous additional health benefits, making it easy to start. Aside from the fact that it doesn't require a lot of equipment and can be done anywhere, running is an excellent method to stay motivated. Finding a jogging partner or changing up your exercises regularly will help you stay motivated when you're having difficulty getting started.

P

NAZARÉ
META

CHAPTER 8

The Risks and Benefits of Running During Pregnancy

During pregnancy, maintaining an active lifestyle can help you feel more energized, improve your mood, and lower your chance of developing pregnancy problems. However, when you consider the various ways in which you might maintain your physical fitness throughout your pregnancy, you might find yourself wondering whether or not it is safe to run.

Because running is such an intense exercise, it is normal that you would be a little afraid to continue doing it while carrying a child. The best part is that you don't have to stop running just yet, so you can keep wearing your running shoes for the time being. However, before pounding the pavement, you should familiarize yourself with the following information on running while pregnant.

Since I'm pregnant, is it safe for me to go for a run?

Friends and family members who mean well may try to dissuade you from running. It's possible that some people would wonder whether the amount of severity is likely to bring on labor early or, even worse, cause issues during pregnancy. On the other hand, if you are made aware of these problems regularly by other people or questioned about them, you could decide to err on the side of caution and quit jogging. Even though the advice and concern mentioned here are offered with the best intentions, it is generally safe for pregnant women to continue their normal activities, including running.

You do not need to worry that running will cause you to miscarry or harm your unborn child. Since you were a runner before becoming pregnant, it is a good idea for you to resume your regular jogging program.

You should pay attention to your body and consider taking specific preventative measures, which will be discussed below.

There is no escaping the reality that your current exercise regimen will change in some way due to your pregnancy. You may need to run at a slower speed or reduce the number of times per week that you do so, but there's no way you'll have to stop running altogether.

What if you were never much of a runner before you got pregnant? Are you able to start running right now?

Finding a method to incorporate some physical activity into your daily routine can have a significant impact, even if you weren't someone who worked out regularly before you were pregnant. Running, on the other hand, is not something you should start doing while pregnant.

Your body is already adapting to the increased workload and undergoing a great deal of change. It is not ideal to begin a rigorous workout because this adds more physical stress to your life.

Choose less strenuous kinds of physical activity, such as light aerobics, strolling, yoga, or the use of low-intensity cardiovascular equipment, such as a treadmill or elliptical trainer. To establish a habit, you should begin softly and steadily build up both the duration and intensity of your workouts.

Take a daily stroll for five minutes as an example, and then gradually work your way up to ten, twenty, and thirty minutes.

Advantages of maintaining a healthy fitness level when pregnant

It is important to remember that although pregnancy is a beautiful experience, it may wreak havoc on your body. You may experience weariness, pregnancy brain fog, mood fluctuations, and, of course, natural weight increase. On the other hand, maintaining a dynamic lifestyle throughout pregnancy can considerably improve how you feel physically and emotionally.

Acrobatic exercise of moderate intensity for at least 150 minutes per week is advised for women during pregnancy, as stated by the American College of Obstetricians and Gynecologists (ACOG). Among these types of exercises is jogging, which works to both speed up your heart rate and make you sweat. Unless you were active before you became pregnant, continuing that exercise during your pregnancy shouldn't offer too many challenges for you (you know, besides the morning sickness, exhaustion, and aches and pains). All you need to do may be readjust the level of difficulty of your workouts and the expectations you have for yourself along the way.

You will have fulfilled the recommendation for 150 minutes of physical activity if you can exercise for five days, each consisting of thirty minutes. It is perfectly acceptable to spend this time jogging; however, you should also try incorporating other activities into your routines, such as walking, swimming, or yoga.

Exercising throughout pregnancy can help alleviate constipation, back discomfort, and exhaustion and promote a healthy weight and a healthy weight overall. Additionally, it minimizes the possibility of developing gestational diabetes and preeclampsia.

Endorphin production in the body is boosted by physical activity, another vital point to keep in mind. All of those are hormones that make you feel happy and can help lift your mood. When pregnant, there is nothing to lose and everything to gain by getting some exercise. You can improve both your physical and emotional health with its assistance.

What are the potential risks associated with running while pregnant?

Even though running is an excellent method to stay active during pregnancy, there is still a possibility that you could face some difficulties. Once you're pregnant, your body will undergo many changes, and one of those adjustments is likely to be a difference in where your center of gravity is located and how well you balance as your belly gets bigger. This puts you in greater danger of falling, especially if you run on trails that aren't perfectly even.

To lower your chances of getting wounded in an accident, you should limit your running to paved surfaces, such as the sidewalk or the track at a nearby school. Additionally, running on level surfaces is easier on your joints, resulting in more pleasant runs for the runner.

When you are in your second and third trimesters of pregnancy, you may find that the bouncing motion is becoming increasingly uncomfortable. On the other hand, one could try wearing a belly support band to minimize this movement.

Be mindful that as your pregnancy progresses, your joints and your ligaments will get looser. This is because your body produces the hormone relaxin to prepare the pelvic ligaments for birthing.

This hormone relaxes the ligaments and joints throughout the body, increasing the likelihood that you will sustain an injury.

It's best to take things slowly at first and steer clear of routines that make you uncomfortable. Changing up your usual routine is not in the least bit frowned upon. It's possible you won't be able to run as far, for as long, or as fast as you usually would as your due date approaches. You might be required to give up running altogether at some time during your pregnancy, at least until after you have given birth to your child, depending on the situation's specifics. Headaches, chest pain, muscle weakness, vaginal bleeding, calf pain, and leaks of amniotic fluid are among the symptoms that indicate you should stop running and make an appointment with your OB-GYN.

Advice on how to be safe while running while pregnant

The following are a few pointers that should make running while pregnant both simpler and safer:

- Invest in the proper pair of running shoes. Your running shoes should provide adequate support for your arches and ankles and fit you well. This maintains the stability of your feet and protects you from falls and injuries. As your body changes throughout pregnancy, you may find that you eventually require a new pair of shoes.

- Put on a supportive sports bra. During pregnancy, your breasts may grow more prominent, making certain activities, such as running, uncomfortable for you. Runners who experience breast soreness can consider purchasing a high-quality sports bra with plenty of support.

- Make sure you're wearing a belly band.

These bands assist in stabilizing a growing belly, reducing the pain or discomfort produced by a tummy that bounces too much. Support bands help improve posture and relieve pressure on the pelvic region.

- Keep hydrated.

Consume a large amount of water not just before but also during and after your workouts to prevent dehydration and overheating. When it's hot and humid outside, another way to keep yourself from overheating is to exercise indoors and wear loose-fitting clothes.

- Be aware of the signals that your body is telling you.

Keeping active throughout pregnancy is beneficial, but it's vital to avoid overdoing it. It is OK to skip an exercise or cut it short if you feel you have gone too far or are too exhausted. If you feel uneasy when you are out jogging, change your exercise to walking.

Include resistance training in your routine.

Because you have a higher risk of injuring your muscles and joints, you should engage in strength training to make your muscles and joints more resilient. The lunge, the squat, and some mild weightlifting are included in these workouts.

- You should only run in areas that have bathrooms.

Because of your baby's increasing weight, the strain on your bladder may increase, causing you to urinate more frequently than usual. This is perfectly normal. Create a running route that is either closer to your house or in an area with public bathrooms.

- Try to maintain a balanced diet.

When you exercise while pregnant, your body has an increased requirement for calories. A pre-workout snack, such as a piece of fruit or toast with nut butter, will help you maintain your energy level to get the most out of your workouts. Consuming foods with a high percentage of water will help keep you hydrated. In addition, ensure that you refuel properly following your workouts by consuming between one and two servings each of carbohydrates and proteins as well as one dish of healthy fat.

Takeaway

Running, as well as other forms of exercise, can benefit your physical and mental health during pregnancy. It can help alleviate back discomfort, reduce constipation, improve mood swings, and assist in the maintenance of a healthy weight for a pregnant woman. Running and other forms of exercise may become more challenging as the pregnancy progresses and you reach further along in the process. Even if you cannot maintain the same speed, engaging in any amount of physical activity is preferable to none. Therefore, you should think about walking, swimming, or other light workouts for at least thirty minutes five days a week rather than jogging or running.

CHAPTER 9

The Importance of Strength Training for Runners

Strength training benefits runners of all experience levels, whether they have just started or have been competing for years. Because they believe that strength training will make them sluggish and unwieldy, many runners shy away from it. On the other hand, participating in strength training sessions can make your running program more efficient and fun.

The Numerous Advantages of Weightlifting for Runners

Strength training can assist you in achieving your goals of being faster, stronger, or leaner. It can also help you reach your goal of losing weight. Your running program can benefit in various ways from engaging in strength training. Here are some of those ways.

Increased Productivity While Running

Strength training is something you should consider doing if you've noticed that your form starts to deteriorate as you become tired after a long run or race. You may enhance and maintain your running form by strengthening your core, ultimately leading to increased running efficiency on your part. Because even slight increases in efficiency can significantly impact a long race, such as a half or full marathon, it is especially vital for individuals preparing for such a race to pay attention to this point.

Weight Loss

As a result of increasing your lean muscle mass, your metabolism will speed up, and you will burn more calories at rest while indulging in physical activity. A significant number of runners have discovered that supplementing their running routine with strength training benefits their overall weight loss efforts and assists them in breaking through weight loss plateaus.

Increased Endurance While Showing Decreases in Fatigue

If you engage in strength training, your body will be better able to endure the stresses of running. Jogging will be easier for you to do correctly since your muscles can perform for a more extended period before becoming fatigued. This practice will help you keep your form as you are running.

Strength training will assist you in avoiding "hitting the wall" or tightening up during the latter parts of a long-distance marathon by giving you the ability to finish the race strong.

Faster Pace

Your overall speed will increase as a direct result of your improved form and your increased endurance. When runners incorporate strength training into their routines, they typically begin to see gains in their race timings within a reasonable amount of time. It is not necessary to devote a significant amount of time to performing strengthening activities. A more significant amount of lean muscle mass can be built with as few as two or three strength-training sessions lasting 15 to 20 minutes each week.

Reduced Potential for Physical Harm

Exercises focusing on the lower body and the core are necessary to lower the probability of injury. You can keep your proper running form for a more extended period if you have more robust core and leg muscles. This will reduce the possibility that you will develop lower back discomfort or any other problems related to bad running form.

Muscle imbalances and weaknesses are the root cause of most running injuries, particularly those that affect the knees and hips. A sports physician or a physical therapist can offer targeted exercises for you to perform if you are experiencing pain, are concerned about a biomechanical fault, or have previously suffered an injury. Aside from the obvious advantage of avoiding discomfort, avoiding injury also ensures that you will maintain your motivation to continue running, increase your chances of developing a regular running routine, and improve your running ability.

Mistakes that runners frequently make put them at risk for injury.

When you start to feel more comfortable, running becomes a more fun activity. If you increase the strength of your leg muscles, you can run for longer durations without suffering signs of fatigue. Running and strength training should not be done on the same day, especially for beginners, who should try to avoid doing both activities on the same day.

Different Variations of Strength Training

There are numerous approaches to building strength, and runners shouldn't assume that all of these approaches are equivalent in value. For example, powerlifting necessitates training such that competitors can lift considerable weight ranging from one to three repetitions at a time. Since this type of training almost always results in significant increases in muscle mass (hypertrophy), it's possible that it's not the best strategy for a runner who wishes to keep their physique trim.

Strength training comes in many forms, but not all are suggested for runners. Those whose primary objective is to increase their running performance should look for training regimens emphasizing workouts that use only one's body weight, functional training, and endurance strength training.

Training for Endurance and Strength

By lowering the amount of weight lifted and increasing the number of repetitions completed, the purpose of endurance strength training is to build muscle endurance.

This type of training requires you to lift approximately 70 percent of your one-rep max and do anywhere from 12 to 20 repetitions. It's possible that you'll complete anything from one to three sets of each activity.

How to Figure Out Your One-Rep Maximum in Functional Training

Running is not the only sport that requires essential bodyweight training. Exercises that are considered to be part of functional training are the lunge and the single-leg squat. Both of these exercises need the large muscles in your body to cooperate like they do during other daily activities such as jogging. Your running gait and overall performance will benefit from the improvements in balance, coordination, and movement efficiency that these exercises provide.

In addition to lowering your risk of injury, functional training can improve your performance.

Examples of Workouts for Functional Training

Plyometrics

Researchers have found that strength training routines incorporating plyometrics can increase a runner's ability to run at a quicker pace and shorten the total amount of time they need to run. Jumping and other activities that entail short, powerful bursts of movement are examples of plyometric exercises.

Try:

Squat jumps

Lunge jumps

Box leaps

Drills involving laterally jumping with a jump rope

Exercises for Plyometric Jumping and Landings

How to Pick the Appropriate Program

There are a few various alternatives available to you when it comes to selecting a weight training program to follow. If you want to increase your running performance, on the other hand, you should select a workout regimen that is personalized to your present fitness level. This will reduce the likelihood that you will experience an injury while you are running. For example, Endurance strength training and Functional training are options worth considering for everybody, regardless of their current fitness level. Almost every exercise can be adapted to accommodate exercisers of varying experience levels, from beginners to experts.

Plyometrics: these are more advanced exercises and have a higher risk of injury because of their more complex nature. These exercises indeed have the potential to be beneficial, but people with more experience should be the ones to perform them.

It's possible that endurance training with weights is not the ideal choice for people who cannot go to the gym regularly or don't have access to this equipment at home. But, conversely, exercises focusing on one's body's weight can be performed virtually anywhere with minimal or no equipment.

Nineteen exercises using one's body weight may be done at home and are suitable for a quick workout. According to research conducted on the advantages of strength training for runners, a consistent training regimen is required to notice effects. Although physical activity daily is not essential, it is recommended that you train for several days each week.

In an extensive analysis of the evidence, the authors concluded that resistance training twice or three times per week for eight to twelve weeks was the most effective strategy for runners. Naturally, this necessitates you strike a balance in your training routine to find time to both jog and work out in the weight room.

Practice on the Days That You Have Off

An intelligent strategy will be to perform weight training on the days you don't run if you don't run every day. Although it is essential to give your muscles time to recover, endurance strength training does not put as much strain on them like other forms of weight lifting, such as powerlifting. Additionally, most exercises for endurance training and functional training help you enhance the range of motion in your joints, which boosts the recovery process.

Another tactic is to undertake strength training on the same days as rigorous running exercises, immediately after or later on the same day. This can be done either immediately after or later in the day. Thanks to this technique, you can recuperate entirely by taking the next day off. On the other hand, it is not something you should do after your long run.

How to Recuperate Properly after Your Marathon: Train like a Champion on your Days off from Running

While it would seem contradictory to undertake strength training after a strenuous workout (like intervals, hills, or tempo), doing strength training on a day when you are not working out will be more beneficial. At the end of your runs, you might also add some exercises focusing on core strength and functional movement. You may, for instance, follow your running workout by performing five minutes of the plank exercise, several different lunge variations, and some single-leg squats before moving on to the stretching portion of your routine.

There is no one approach superior to another when it comes to incorporating strength training into your routine; however, it is essential to be consistent. To get the most out of your strength training, select a program you can stick to consistently.

How to Make Your Strength Training More Effective

Common Mistakes

The following are some of the most common errors that runners make when lifting weights.

Too Much Too Soon

When runners decide to add strength training to their routine, one of the most common mistakes is that they start by doing too much, too soon. Many runners have a competitive mindset, which can cause them to attempt activities with more significant weight or a higher level of difficulty than they are capable of, which can have disastrous consequences. Keep in mind that the purpose of your program is to make you a faster and more capable runner. Being overly competitive in the weight room (lifting too much weight and performing excessive reps) can lead to injury and tiredness, which can keep you from running for several days.

How to Stay Consistent in Your Running Routine: One of the Most Common Mistakes New Runners Make

Another typical error is inconsistent training. There is a low probability that your running performance will improve if you commit to an effective weight training program but only complete the program once every few weeks. It's possible that doing so puts you in danger of getting hurt. Instead, you might think about beginning on a modest scale and expanding gradually. On your days off or at the end of your runs, commit to doing 15 to 20 minutes of stretching. Maintain a regular workout schedule, and add additional training if time permits.

Getting Started

Do you not know where to start? The following categories of physical activity are beneficial for runners:

Exercises targeting the lower body include lunges, squats, donkey kicks, and wall squats.

Planks, crunches, bridges, V-sits, and back extensions are examples of exercises that strengthen the core.

Exercises for the upper body include:

- The tricep dip.
- The overhead tricep extension.
- The overhead shoulder press.
- The pushup.

Pick out a few easy exercises to perform to get started. Then, make sure you stick to your training schedule to lessen your chances of getting hurt and have a more satisfying running experience.

A regular program of strength training will greatly aid a runner's ability to improve and achieve success in the sport. You should keep this in mind whether you are training for a marathon or are just beginning your jogging routine. Gia Alvarez, a professional marathoner, and owner of a treadmill studio in Tenafly, New Jersey, is quoted as saying, "Running is not a lateral movement, and while it utilizes numerous muscle groups, it requires a mind-body connection to engage your muscles correctly while you are running." "Strength training on all different planes can help you connect to your muscles and strengthen the weak ones. Strength training on the appropriate muscle areas can improve your running technique, which can help prevent aches and pains.

There are a large number of strength-training routines that may be performed with very little or even no equipment at all, which is an added plus. It is well recognized that exercises such as planks, bridges, and squats develop overall stability. It has been shown that reducing joint pain and the likelihood of damage can be accomplished by supplementing an intense cardio workout with strength training using weights, kettlebells, or resistance bands. It would help if you also observed an increase in your stamina and endurance due to this.

Training for increases in body size is much more complex than you might imagine, even though some people may be concerned that lifting weights will increase muscle bulk that could impede their stride. It is doubtful that you will become the next major heavyweight power-lifter unless you regularly engage in strenuous physical activity and consume significant calories. Using the heaviest barbells to observe and feel progress in your workouts is unnecessary.

You should be able to anticipate a significant improvement in your performance if you work on steadily elevating the difficulty of your workouts. "A strength training session need not take up an entire hour of your time. Alvarez continues her explanation by saying, "Even 10 minutes can make a significant difference." If you would like to learn about the strength-training routines that are most useful for runners to do as a part of their overall training program, continue reading because this chapter will cover them all in detail.

Don't forget to stretch after you've finished your workout; that's important! Even if we spend a lot of time talking about strength training, it is critical to point out that it is necessary to stretch the muscles you utilize after indulging in either strength training or jogging. Before getting into bed, I like to stretch for around 15 minutes. It helps me feel better. According to Alvarez, "going to bed with happy muscles is highly advantageous since a lot of recuperation is done while you sleep, so going to bed with happy muscles is quite good."

Workout Routine for Strength Training That Only Takes 15 Minutes

Select a few exercises for yourself from the ones provided here. Perform each exercise for thirty seconds, making sure to work both sides of your body if necessary. Rest 15 seconds between.

You should try to slow down your heart rate a little bit, but not by an excessive amount.

Perform this sequence of exercises three times in a row.

1. Rows

According to Alvarez, rows are an excellent exercise to perform to build strength in the muscles of the upper back. When you run, you must ensure that your upper back is engaged to keep your ribs and lungs from becoming compressed.

Instructions: On a mat, get on your hands and knees while maintaining a neutral spine position, and grasp light to medium weights in both hands. Position yourself as described here.

Repeat the movement by bringing each arm up one at a time, pulling your shoulder blades together as you do so. Upon completing the prescribed number of repetitions on one arm, move on to the opposite arm.

2. Extensions with the Stability Ball

By performing this technique, you will strengthen your lower back but also aid in maintaining a solid core. As Alvarez describes them, these extensions work the entire back, proving that the core consists of more than the abdominals.

Step one: Lying on your back on a stability ball with the ball under your stomach and hips is the starting position for this exercise.

The second step is to ensure that all your toes are firmly planted on the ground.

Step three entails performing steps one and two once more. You should lift your upper body a few inches off the ground while holding your hands behind your head. As long as you can, hold this position. While doing this, you should draw your shoulder blades together and engage your upper back in the yoga pose known as the upward-facing dog.

3. Lateral Band Walks while Driving Your Arms Forward

This multi-joint exercise can help you build strength in your shoulders, hips, and glutes.

Using the resistance band for the side-to-side movements is one of Alvarez's favorite aspects of this activity because it also serves as an excellent exercise for strengthening hip and knee stability.

Instructions: Using a resistance band, wrap it around both legs, so it sits on the lower to the middle portion of your thighs and just above your knees. Place some light weights in both hands and stand with your feet shoulder-width apart. As you walk sideways while maintaining the tension on the band, get into a squat position by pushing your knees to a 45-degree angle. Continue this movement. While moving your feet, your arms should be flailing back and forth like you are racing.

4. Kettlebell Swings

As much as we use the arms for the swing, it concentrates on the lower body, according to Alvarez.

So even though we use the arms for the swing, it is about having complete body control.

This is a full-body workout since you have to activate your glutes, lower abdominals, quads, and hamstrings to control the movement of the kettlebell. It would help if you consciously contract your glutes at the highest point of the swing.

Step one: You should stand with your feet hip-width apart, your knees slightly bent, and your toes pointed forward. This position is called the "hip-distance" stance.

Step two: Put a kettlebell with a weight that is comfortable for you between your legs. If you do not have access to a kettlebell, you can perform the exercises with any weight that falls between medium and heavy between your legs. Get into a squatting position and grab the kettlebell with both hands (bending your knees to lower your body). Put your hips in front of you and bring the kettlebell to your chest. Take control of the swing and bring it back down to the ground.

5. Side Lunge with Overhead Press

The focus of side lunges is on the lower body, and they also work the inner thigh muscle.

The movement of your body from side to side while you perform this exercise helps enhance your stability and balance. When you include the overhead press in your routine, you are now strengthening your shoulders and abdominal muscles.

How to: As a starting point, stand with your feet shoulder-width apart, your toes pointed forward, and a light to medium weight in each of your hands. Side lunge by stepping one foot in front of the other and bending the knee of the leg leading you into the lunge. When you bend forward, keep your hips pulled back almost as much as they would be if you were sitting in a chair.

You can get out of this posture by removing the foot in the lunge and returning to a standing position. Once you are upright, pull your feet together and simultaneously curl your body to force the weights overhead to perform a shoulder press. Reduce the weights, then perform the exercise on the other side.

6. Reverse Crunch

The exercise known as the reverse crunch targets your lower abdominals and your rectus abdominis, which are also referred to as the "six-pack" muscles. Strong lower abdominal muscles support the lower back.

How to: If you want to protect your back while doing this exercise, you should lay down on a mat. It would help if you started lying on your back with your feet flexed and your legs together. After that, you should extend your legs up to the ceiling. Maintain a side-arm stance with your palms planted firmly into the ground. To activate your lower abdominals, bring your belly button into your spine and hold it there. Instead of pointing your toes in the direction of your face, raise your feet so that they are pointed directly up to the ceiling, and raise your hips so that they are 1–2 inches off the ground. This will help you get into the correct position to point your toes.

Once you've held the position for a breath, go back to where you started and do the exercise again.

7. Forearm Plank Hip Dips

When performing hip dips, the abdominals and the obliques are working. It is important to remember to keep your body in a straight line and to keep your core engaged during the entire movement. On a mat, get into a posture where you are doing a forearm plank. Bring one hip closer to the mat while bringing the lower belly toward the spine and keeping a straight line with the rest of the body. Get back into the plank posture on your forearms. On the other side, repeat the process.

8. Dead Bug Toe Touch

Because a dead bug engages all of the abdominal muscles, it is one of Alvarez's all-time favorite exercises for the abdominal region. When it comes to this particular exercise, the slower you go, the better because the focus should be on controlling your core.

How to: Place yourself on a mat and roll over onto your back to protect your neck and back.

Raise your legs up until they form a 90-degree angle with the rest of your body. Make sure that your knees are aligned perfectly above your hips, and that your arms are reaching as far up toward the ceiling as they possibly can. While lowering the opposite leg to the ground, slowly drop one arm behind your head while concurrently reducing the other leg. Maintain a firm press into the mat with your lower back, and then bring both feet back to the beginning position.

On the other side, repeat the same process.

If you want to be a more robust and quicker runner, you should include strength training workouts for runners as a regular component of your training regimen. This is the best way to achieve these goals. When people first start running, one of the most common mistakes is to ignore all other forms of physical activity and focus solely on running. Although beginning with this strategy is not a bad idea, if you are genuinely committed to improving your strength and speed, you will need to incorporate ancillary work such as strength training into your overall training regimen.

CHAPTER 10

Best Ways to Prevent and Treat the Most Common Running Injuries

Running has grown in popularity to maintain and improve one's physical fitness. According to a Trusted Source, more than 40 million people in the United States run regularly. Even while running is a terrific way to stay fit, many runners will experience some injury at some point in their careers. More than 80 percent of all running injuries are caused by repetitive stress, yet others, like sprains and tears, can occur without warning. Running injuries, symptoms, and treatment options are all described in this chapter.

Concerning running-related injuries

If you're a runner like many others, you might rack up hundreds or even thousands of kilometers each year. As a result, your muscles, joints, and connective tissue might suffer damage from the constant impact of your feet striking the ground repeatedly. According to a summary of previous research published in 2015 (Trustworthy Source), runners are most likely to get injuries to their feet, knees, and legs.

The following is a breakdown of the location-specific incidence of running injuries that are provided in the review:

7.2 to 50 percent for the knees

9.0 to 32.2% of the total for the lower leg

Upper leg: 3.4 to 38.1 percent

Foot: somewhere between 5.7 and 39.3 percent

3.9 to 16.6 percent for the ankles

3.3 to 11.5 percent of cases are located in the hips, pelvis, or groin.

5.3% to 19.1% of cases include the lower back.

Let's take a more in-depth look at a few running injuries that crop up the most frequently.

1. Runner's knee (patellofemoral syndrome)

Patellofemoral syndrome is another name for runner's knee, which describes discomfort in the front of the knee or the kneecap. Athletes frequently suffer from the condition known as runner's knee. Runner's knee is a broad word. Overuse injuries like this are common in sports like running and leaping, where those movements are repeated frequently. A runner's knee may be more likely to develop in those with weak hips or the muscles surrounding their knees.

Runner's knee can be painful and cause these symptoms:

A dull ache that can be felt in either knee and can vary from minor discomfort to severe agony

Worsens with extended sitting or worsens while running, climbing stairs, or squatting for extended periods

Cracking or popping sounds may also be heard as a symptom of this type of injury after the victim has been immobile for an extended time

A physical exam is usually sufficient for a doctor to diagnose a runner's knee, but they could suggest getting an X-ray to rule out any other diseases. To treat a runner's knee injury, a physical therapist can provide you with a specific therapy plan to follow.

2. Tendinitis of the Achilles

Achilles tendinitis is a tendon inflammation that extends from your calf muscle down to your heel. This tendon connects your lower leg's calf muscle to the heel. It may occur when you increase the distance you run or the speed you run. If you have Achilles tendinitis and let it go untreated, you put yourself at an increased risk of rupturing your Achilles tendon. If this tendon is ruptured, surgical intervention is typically necessary to heal it.

The following are examples of symptoms that are frequently experienced by patients who have Achilles tendinitis:

Aching at the back of your lower leg, just above your heel, swelling in the area of your Achilles tendon

A restricted range of motion while flexing your foot toward your shin, a warm sensation over the tendon of your foot

3. IT band syndrome

You have an IT band that runs from the outside of your hip to the outside of your knee, and it's referred to as your iliotibial band or your IT band. When you walk or run, this band of tissue helps to support your knee, which can help prevent injuries. The irritation from the IT band repeatedly pressing against the leg bone is known as IT band syndrome. Because of their tight IT bands, runners have a high incidence of this condition. This issue may also be exacerbated by weak gluteal muscles, weak abdominal muscles, or weak hip muscles.

IT band syndrome manifests as a stabbing pain on the outside aspect of the affected leg, typically located just above the knee. It's also possible that your IT band is sensitive to the touch. When you bend your knee, the discomfort will typically become more severe.

4. Shin splints

Pain that is felt in the front of the inside sections of the lower legs, along the shinbone, is referred to as shin splints. Another name for this condition is tibial stress syndrome. Shin splints are an injury that can occur if you increase the amount of running that you do too quickly, mainly if you run on hard surfaces. For the most part, Shin splints are not significant injuries and can be cured by resting the affected leg. However, they can progress into a stress fracture if not treated.

The following symptoms could accompany shin splints:

A dull ache running along the front of the innersection of your shinbone; pain that gets worse when you move, soreness to the touch, slight swelling

Shin splints can typically be alleviated by resting the affected leg or reducing the time spent running or the distance covered.

5. Hamstring injuries

During the portion of the running cycle known as the swing, your hamstrings are responsible for slowing down your lower leg. Your hamstrings may be more prone to damage if they are tired, tight, or both. Distance runners do not typically find themselves in the position of experiencing a quick hamstring strain compared to sprinters. Most of the time, distance runners will suffer from hamstring strains that develop gradually and are brought on by repetitive tiny tears in the muscle fibers and connective tissue of the hamstring.

If you have injured your hamstring, you may suffer the following symptoms:

A dull discomfort in the back of your upper leg, a hamstring muscle that is painful to the touch, as well as weakness and stiffness in your hamstring

6. Plantar fasciitis

One of the most frequent types of foot injuries is called plantar fasciitis. A thick layer of tissue known as fascia on the bottom of the foot can become inflamed or degenerate due to this condition. When you walk or run, this layer of tissue works like a spring to help you absorb impact. The fascia in your legs can experience additional stress if you ramp up the amount of jogging you do too rapidly. You are more likely to develop plantar fasciitis if you have tight muscles in your calves or if your calves are weak.

Typical symptoms consist of the following:

Having pain in the arch or the heel of your foot

Pain that comes on gradually

A burning sensation on the bottom of your foot

Pain that is worse in the morning

Pain that comes on after you've been on your feet for a while

Pain that comes on after you've been active for a long time

7. Stress fractures

Hairline cracks in the bone result from repeated stress or impact. Stress fractures can occur in any bone in your body. In runners, stress fractures most frequently appear in the midfoot, the heel, or the lower leg. The ball of the foot and the lower leg are also familiar places. If you have any cause to suspect that you may have suffered a stress fracture in your bone, you should make an appointment with a qualified medical practitioner as soon as possible. To identify a stress fracture, they need to take an X-ray.

The following are some of the typical symptoms of a stress fracture:

Fractures can cause swelling, bruising, or discomfort in the area where the fracture is located, as well as pain that worsens over time from something that was scarcely noticeable at first. Healing from a stress fracture can take anywhere from six to eight weeks, and during that time, you might need to use crutches or a cast to keep the bone in place.

8. Ankle sprain

Sprained ankles result from excessive straining of the ligaments that connect the leg to the ankle. Sprains are typical injuries that can be sustained when a person lands on the outer aspect of their foot and rolls their ankle simultaneously.

Common symptoms connected with an ankle sprain include:

Discoloration, pain, edema, and bruising

Restricted mobility throughout the body

To get the best outcomes from treating an ankle sprain, you should try to get plenty of rest, practice self-care, and/or participate in physical therapy. It could take a runner several weeks or even months to fully recover from this type of injury.

Different kinds of running injuries also exist. Other common types of injuries suffered by runners include the following:

An infection of the toenail. An ingrown toenail is a medical term for a situation in which the side of your nail grows into the skin surrounding your toe. If it becomes infected, it may cause pain and inflammation along with the toenail, and pus may leak out of it.

Bursitis. The fluid-filled sacs called bursae are found beneath the muscles and tendons of your body. They contribute to the lubrication of your joints in some way. Running can irritate the hip or the area surrounding the knee if you run in a way that causes repeated rubbing against these sacs.

Meniscal tear.

A tear in the cartilage found in your knee is referred to as a meniscal tear. It frequently gives you the feeling that your joint is locking up.

The syndrome of the anterior compartment

When the muscles in the front of your lower leg put pressure on the nerves and blood vessels in that area, a condition known as anterior compartment syndrome can develop. This syndrome has the potential to be a life-threatening situation.

Stress on the calf

Running can cause calf strains, often called strained calves, which can be painful and require medical attention.

Different kinds of treatment for running injuries

It is crucial to follow up with your primary care physician if you are experiencing pain, discomfort, or difficulty running to obtain an accurate diagnosis and rule out the potential that your symptoms are caused by another ailment.

Treatment often consists of the following for many common running injuries:

Sessions of physical therapy as well as exercises that are specialized and follow the RICE protocol (rest, ice, compression, elevation)

Using nonsteroidal anti-inflammatory medications (NSAIDs) such as aspirin or ibuprofen

Reducing the amount of time spent running as well as the distance you cover

Other, more specialized treatments could consist of the following:

For runners' knees, try exercising your quadriceps and hip muscles, extending any tight quads or calves, and consider investing in a pair of orthotic shoes. Calves should be stretched and massaged to treat Achilles tendinitis. Stretching your IT bands every day and working on strengthening your hip muscles can help treat IT band syndrome. Changing your running style, strengthening your glutes, and stretching and strengthening your hamstrings are all effective treatments for hamstring problems. Calves should be stretched and strengthened to treat plantar fasciitis. For stress fractures, treatment options include a cast, crutches, or surgery. Ankle strengthening exercises are recommended for patients with sprained ankles.

Advice on how to avoid getting hurt

Anyone can sustain an injury when running. However, the following advice can help you lower your chances of getting hurt:

Acclimate yourself.

Before beginning to run, ensure that you have properly warmed up by going for a light jog or performing dynamic mobility stretches for five to ten minutes, such as an arm or leg swings.

Gradually increase the distance you are running.

The 10 percent rule is one that many runners stick to, which states that they never increase the amount of running they do in a week by more than 10 percent at a time.

Take care of injuries that have been bothering you.

If you have a nagging injury, you should rest it as soon as possible to prevent it from becoming a more serious problem.

Your physical therapist will provide an accurate diagnosis and a treatment plan tailored to your specific needs.

Work on your technique

Running incorrectly can strain your muscles and joints, especially if you run for long distances. Improving your running technique can be as simple as working with a running coach or as involved as taping yourself jogging.

Work on improving your hip strength

To better protect your knees and ankles, you should incorporate stability exercises like glute bridges and single-leg squats into your workout routine.

Make use of surfaces with a softer texture

Running on surfaces that are softer on your joints, such as grass, rubber tracks, sand, or gravel, is preferable to running on pavement. If you're struggling with a persistent injury, you should try running on a cushioned surface until the pain subsides.

Think about participating in several types of workouts

Your joints need a break from the consistent strain of running, and adding low-impact workouts like cycling or swimming to your program will assist and increase your aerobic fitness while providing your joints a rest from the force of running.

The Final Details

At some time in their careers, most runners will battle with an injury. Your knees, legs, and feet are the areas of your body most likely to suffer an injury from running. If you have any form of pain or discomfort after running, you should make an appointment with your primary care physician as soon as possible to get an accurate diagnosis of your condition. Recovery from many common running injuries can be aided by following the RICE procedure, taking non-steroidal anti-inflammatory drugs (NSAIDs)for pain, following a physical therapy plan, and engaging in focused workouts. Running less frequently and for shorter distances can also help you recover from your runs more quickly.

To recover fully from a running injury, you will need a significant amount of time and patience, which is frequently challenging to find. Most runners will, at some point or another throughout their training, go through some level of discomfort when running. These strenuous workouts don't always feel like they're going well, and finishing up long runs can frequently result in aches that have never been experienced before. When your annoyance develops into actual pain, it is time for you to give yourself a breather and concentrate on getting better.

It is generally required to take time off from running, get lots of rest, and undertake specific strengthening activities to treat running injuries. This treatment approach is a combination of things not very high on a runner's list of activities they find pleasurable. To treat running injuries, taking time off from running is often necessary, getting plenty of rest, and performing targeted strengthening exercises. The ability to recover from a running injury correctly can be the deciding factor in whether you have your best training season yet or whether you end up being chronically injured.

Use these six measures to recuperate from a running injury and return to running in better health and with greater strength than you were previously capable of.

How to Get Back on Your Feet after a Running Injury

Spend some time doing absolutely nothing.

Running through pain, whether you already have a running injury or are on the verge of developing one, is the worst thing you can do if you are injured from running. To avoid worsening things and getting better, it is essential to take some time off at the first symptom of a running injury. It is not always easy to take time off while you are in the thick of a good training cycle or a running season, but if you take a few days off immediately, it may help you avoid taking a long hiatus in the future. Taking some time off to recover after an injury is the first stage in the healing process. It would help if you skipped your workouts for a few days so that you may concentrate on obtaining plenty of rest instead. During the first few days of your hiatus, you should try to rest as much as possible and spend as little time moving around.

The first few days of resting are entirely the most important to getting well, but as time goes on and your running injury starts to get better, you'll be able to start incorporating different kinds of cross-training to get back in shape.

Perform strengthening workouts consistently.

When you are trying to recover from a running injury, the first thing that you should do is make sure you get plenty of rest. Finding out what led to your injury is the second most critical thing you should do, and once you have that information, you should take steps to prevent it from happening again. Most of the time, running injuries are brought on by either a lack of strength in the muscles, an imbalance between the forces, excessive use, or improper form. It is helpful to narrow down the possible causes of the ailment to devise a strategy for your rehabilitation.

If you are merely dealing with a localized soreness or fracture, you must work to strengthen the muscles that surround the affected area to make a full recovery. Examine your form and technique to see what went wrong and how to avoid it happening again if you've strained or twisted something. After identifying and isolating the source of your ailment, you should engage in exercises that constitute physical therapy or rehabilitation to strengthen the muscles in the affected region. You will need to perform the isolation exercises daily to build the appropriate strength and ensure that you do not sustain another injury once you resume running.

Reduce your workload by engaging in additional cross-training.

As soon as the discomfort has subsided, the need to immediately resume everyday workout routines at full strength is understandable. Nevertheless, it is vital to ease back into it in an organized manner, and this recommendation applies regardless of how long you were away from training. After a period of complete relaxation that lasts for several days, weeks, or months, you must start carefully with low mileage. During this time, you should compensate for your lack of fitness by engaging in more cross-training. This will assist your body to go back to its previous level of fitness.

To assist your body to get back into running shape, choose low-impact cross-training or strength training such as yoga or Pilates. Stay away from anything that can cause discomfort or strain your injuries just when it starts to heal. When starting your new exercise routine, you should focus more on cross-training than jogging. You can progressively increase your running mileage while simultaneously reducing the time spent on cross-training until you are back to your regular workout regimen if you successfully avoid injury for an extended period.

Check that your form, as well as your posture, are correct.

When trying to get over a running injury, this is the ideal moment to pay a little more attention to your form and posture. The improper shape or muscular imbalance that results from running can be traced back to the source of many running ailments. This can cause specific muscles to become weaker while others become overworked.

Take advantage of the fact that you will be running fewer miles and at a more relaxed pace when you return to running to focus more intently on your form and posture. As you start running again, you should examine your muscles for any muscle imbalances and carefully inventory your running technique.

A fantastic way to check for any posture problems you might not be aware of while running is to take pictures of yourself or record yourself doing the activity. When you resume jogging, pay close attention to your form, stride, and cadence, and give yourself plenty of time to build healthy routines that you can carry forward. Please make the most of your time off to concentrate on the less critical aspects of your training to perform them efficiently once you get back into the swing of things.

Take things gradually and not too quickly.

It might be aggravating to stop jogging because of an injury and be forced to take some time off. Regardless of where they are in their training regimen or why they are running in the first place, runners regularly report feeling confused and annoyed when unanticipated changes occur to their training schedules. This is the case regardless of the motivation behind their jogging.

It is tempting to immediately resume all of your previous training once you have reached a point where you are healthy and free of pain. However, we tend to hasten our recovery a little bit because it is such a thrilling experience to get the green light to start running again after being sidelined for several weeks or months. Remember that just because the pain in your leg has subsided or your physician has permitted you to try jogging again, this does not mean that you will be able to pick up exactly where you left off.

You are going to need some time as well as patience to go back to the distance and pace that you were previously at. It's best to ease back into running gradually, taking it easy and putting off strength training until after you've built up a strong foundation in the sport. You need to slow down and concentrate on the fact that you can still run. Your patience will be tested during the recovery process from a running injury; nevertheless, taking it slow will enable your body to return even more potent than before the injury.

Put an end to it at the first hint of pain.

When you start to run again after recovering from an injury, one of the most crucial things to keep in mind is to stop at the first sign of any pain. Your body will tell you it has not yet fully recovered from an illness or injury by letting you know through the pain sensation that it is doing so. Therefore, if you feel anything, even the slightest bit of discomfort, you should either slow down what you're doing or stop altogether. It is never a good idea to push oneself through suffering. You should immediately stop running and give yourself an extra day or two off if you suffer from any soreness. Occasionally, the last bit of discomfort from your injury can be alleviated with only a few more days of rest.

CHAPTER 11

The Benefits of Running for Mental Health

The term "runner's high" refers to a fleeting but profoundly euphoric feeling resulting from strenuous physical activity. Popular culture attributes this mood to certain chemicals. You've probably felt that wonderful sense of calm that comes after a vigorous workout. The sensation, sometimes referred to as a "runner's high," is primarily associated with an increase in endorphins released after engaging in physical activity. But are you experiencing an endorphin rush, or is something else going on here?

A Guide to Achieving a Runner's High Through These Tips

Switching up your regular jogging routine can increase your likelihood of experiencing the euphoric state known as "runner's high."

The following three items are included in the tips:

Get Some Fresh Air and Exercise Your Senses by Going Outside

Compared to people who spend less time outdoors, 120 minutes participating in outdoor activities can experience a 23 percent improvement in their well-being and a 59 percent improvement in their health, according to a study published in Scientific Reports. More than 19,000 people from the United Kingdom participated in this study on working out outside, and the findings were consistent regardless of gender, age, or level of health.

Complete the Run with a Friend

An important finding by the Centers for Disease Control and Prevention, jogging with a partner can motivate you and let you cheer each other on as you cross the finish line together. It can, in turn, produce feelings of positivity and optimism in oneself. Only one of you needs to detect a difference for it to be significant. Running alongside people of varying ages and genders may be an excellent way to boost your motivation, which is why many people find joining a group preferable to going alone when they run.

Take in Some Tunes

Running brings up uncomfortable feelings, but listening to music might help soothe such senses. A research study published in the famous International Journal of Physiology, Pathophysiology, and Pharmacology found that listening to music while exercising can boost one's performance in terms of power and strength and postpone the onset of exhaustion. For this study, fifty people worked out either with or without musical accompaniment. The findings demonstrated that the entire workout duration while using music was noticeably longer than when using the same amount of time when exercising without music.

Running has been shown to have significant positive effects on mental health by releasing endorphins, which give runners a euphoric feeling during and after a run. If you're still looking for a phantom high, you can try a few unconventional methods to help you get there. These tricks include taking your workout outside and running with friends. You can try these techniques if you are still looking for this phantom high. To avoid being hurt while running, you should consult a doctor before starting a new jogging routine. This will ensure that you stay safe.

David Linden, Ph.D., a professor of neuroscience at John Hopkins University School of Medicine, laid forth the high and other effects of running on the brain.

What Happens to Your Brain and the Rest of Your Body When You Go for a Run

When you first start running, a series of physiological changes take place in your body, including the following:

You may find that your breathing becomes heavy and that you experience a quick increase in your pulse rate as your heart pumps more rapidly to deliver oxygenated blood to your muscles and brain. This is because your heart will need to pump blood at a higher rate to meet the increased demand for oxygen that the rest of your body will have. When you get into your groove, your body begins to produce hormones known as endorphins. The term "runner's high" refers to a fleeting but profoundly euphoric feeling resulting from strenuous physical activity. Popular culture attributes this mood to certain chemicals. However, research has shown that runner's high is not all that common, with most athletes claiming they have never experienced it.

According to Linden, "in reality, many distance runners don't feel happy at the finish of a long race; rather, they feel exhausted or even queasy. "Even though endorphins help muscles avoid pain, it is exceedingly unlikely that endorphins in the blood contribute to a pleasurable experience or even a change in mood in the slightest degree. Instead, endorphins prevent muscles from experiencing pain. According to research, endorphins cannot cross the barrier that separates the blood and the brain.

The relaxed sensation you get after a run may be caused by endocannabinoids, which are biological molecules similar to cannabis but are created naturally by the body. According to Linden, physical activity raises the levels of endocannabinoids that are present in the bloodstream. In contrast to endorphins, endocannabinoids have a far easier time traversing the cellular barrier between the bloodstream and the brain. This barrier prevents endorphins from entering the brain. Once absorbed by the brain, neuromodulators that improve mood can provide short-term psychoactive effects, such as a reduction in anxious feelings and a sense of calm.

The Long-Term Benefits of Physical Activity for the Brain

When performed regularly, cardiovascular exercise can stimulate the creation of new blood vessels that supply nourishment to the brain. This means that the mental benefits of running do not end when the activity does. By stimulating a process known as neurogenesis, physical activity has the potential to generate new brain cells in specific regions of the brain. This, in turn, may contribute to an overall improvement in brain performance and help prevent cognitive deterioration.

Linden claims that "exercise has a significant effect on one's mood as an antidepressant." "It reduces the brain's sensitivity to physical and emotional stress," said one researcher. In addition, the volume of the hippocampus, which is the area of the brain connected with memory and learning, has been found to expand in the brains of those who engage in regular physical activity.

The following are additional mental benefits: improved working memory and focus; improved task-switching ability; elevated mood.

Over time, regular cardiovascular exercise like running, jogging, or any other sort of physical activity can help you achieve more than just physical benefits. "The best thing you can do to slow down the decline of your cognitive abilities as you get older is to exercise regularly," says Linden.

Running is beneficial to one's mental health. Running, in addition to helping train the body, can also help train the mind. When you run, you gain the ability to concentrate and the will to push through weariness and challenges along the way. You can strengthen your capacity to endure and triumph over challenges of varying sizes and obtain a fresh perspective on the challenges themselves. Running supports the muscles that allow your body to complete longer distances and strengthens the willpower that propels you to run even when you'd rather miss a workout. This exercise gives you strength that can be applied to other aspects of your life.

Memory

There is some evidence that running can cause alterations within the brain. Researchers examined the brains of competitive distance runners for a study published in the journal Frontiers in Human Neuroscience. Researchers discovered that runners had more significant connections between the frontoparietal network and other brain regions associated with self-control and working memory than non-runners. This was the case compared to runners who did not engage in running. Running is believed by researchers to be beneficial to one's memory since it increases both one's aerobic capacity and the cognitive demands placed on the body.

Cellular Growth

It has been suggested that strenuous physical activity, such as jogging or walking quickly, may increase cellular proliferation in the brain, which in turn helps avoid cognitive loss. The process of creating new neurons in the brain is called neurogenesis, and regular exercise is one of the most critical variables that might influence this process.

According to the findings of a study that was conducted in 2012 and published in the journal Neurology, older adults who engaged in higher levels of physical activity had increased white and gray matter density, less atrophy, and reduced white matter lesions, all of which are typical biomarkers associated with the aging process.

Ability to adapt one's thinking

There is evidence that running may also provide an additional advantage exclusive to the brain. The cognitive flexibility of study participants who engaged in interval running training increased more than those who had a physically active lifestyle. However, this finding was based on a comparison between the two groups. Running affects your ability to switch between mental tasks quickly and effectively. When confronted with challenges, having more cognitive flexibility means that you can rapidly switch gears, adjust to change, and devise new courses of action.

Running Builds Self-Esteem

Running instills a sense of self-assurance in its participants that is unmatched by most other individual sports. Runners gain strength and self-assurance by consistently putting one foot in front of the other. Running gives you a sense of empowerment and independence that comes with knowing that your legs and body are solid and robust. Running allows you to climb hills and clear barriers, and it gives you the ability to do so.

Researchers have established a direct correlation between participating in vigorous physical activities such as running and jogging and having higher levels of self-esteem. Participating in regular physical activity can result in enhanced views of fitness and body image, which are connected to increases in self-esteem.

The evaluation conducted in 2020 also looked at research that focused solely on runners and examined various distances, intensities, and styles of running.

Several studies showed a clear correlation between higher levels of self-identity and self-efficacy and lower levels of depression.

According to a survey, Marathon training has also been linked to improved self-esteem and increased psychological fortitude. Evaluating how far you've gone in terms of the distance you've covered, the amount of time you've spent running, or your overall running abilities can be an incredibly inspiring and self-affirming experience.

Running is an excellent sleep aid.

Running can help you get a good night's sleep, which is connected to more significant mental health. Sleep deprivation can initiate negative mental health states such as stress, anxiety, and depression. In addition, certain mental health illnesses, such as bipolar disorder, can make it more difficult to fall asleep and stay asleep.

To investigate the connection between getting enough exercise and rest, researchers from the National Health and Nutrition Examination Survey (NHANES) in 2005–2006 analyzed the responses of more than 3,000 adults in a study published in 2011. Researchers found that those who met the prescribed levels of physical activity had a risk of experiencing daytime fatigue that was 65 percent lower than those who did not get enough exercise regularly. This was in contrast to the participants who did not acquire adequate physical activity. Those who did not get a good amount of regular exercise were more likely to experience daytime fatigue.

According to Dr. Petkov, excessive running can undoubtedly harm one's health.

The development of an obsession is one indicator that an individual is engaging in excessive running, which can negatively impact mental health. If specific objectives are not achieved, a person may become frustrated or disheartened, resulting in more extreme actions, such as despair and a loss of desire.

— Velimir Petkov, MD

Running too much can result in physical implications such as chronic soreness and exhaustion, leading to irritation, irritability, mood swings, loss of focus, and other emotional symptoms. In addition, running too much can lead to emotional symptoms such as anger, depression, and anxiety. Excessive running can also lead to emotional consequences such as anger, sadness, and lack of focus.

Overtraining syndrome is a condition that can be caused by running too much and whose symptoms include:

- Chronic fatigue.
- Decreased physical performance.
- Loss of appetite.
- Decreased immunity.
- Loss of enthusiasm for exercise.
- Dreading your workouts or runs.

Running too much can lead to overtraining syndrome.

According to Dr. Petkov, there is a danger in doing too much of a good thing.

According to the author, an indication that you may be overdoing it and need a break from jogging is when you stop feeling energized but instead get exhausted..

Like any other activity, running should be done in moderation and with rests in between each run, says Dr. Petkov. Runners who are just starting should focus their attention, particularly on this particular aspect of the sport.

There is no doubt that running is beneficial to the body, but numerous studies have shown that it is also helpful to the mind in a variety of significant ways. Your regular running routine can have a lot of beneficial consequences on your mental health, and these effects can be seen regardless of whether you run for fun or train specifically for marathons.

4684
DOURO

CHAPTER 12

The Importance of Mental Toughness Training for Runners

Regarding long-distance running, your mental toughness and physical endurance can be tested in equal measure. Unfortunately, some runners find that their thoughts cannot keep up with the physical exertion they are putting their bodies through, even though their bodies can run for greater distances.

Try following these ideas if you want to improve your mental fitness for lengthy runs.

1. Talk to Your Mind

Have a conversation with yourself if you're going for a run yourself and find completing the activity challenging. Remind yourself that the exhaustion you feel is merely mental and not physical and that you can overcome this obstacle. Telling oneself things like, "I'll have some water in five minutes; that will make me feel better," is an excellent way to motivate yourself to take action. It can be beneficial to say things to yourself like this.

Practicing thankfulness is another method that can be utilized in self-talk. Remember that running is something you get to do and not something you have to do. Appreciate the fact that you can move and have the stamina to travel for a long-distance, as well as the time, the environment, the weather, and the training you have right now. If you are about to complete the longest run you have ever done, keep in mind how proud you will feel when you reach the end of it.

2. Break Up Your Run

Your run will feel much more manageable if you break it up into smaller parts at specific points along the way. For example, if you plan to run twenty miles, you should tell yourself, "Okay, this is going to be four runs of five miles. "Imagine that at the beginning of each new section, you are simply beginning a recent run with fresh legs, and from that point on, your only focus should be on finishing that segment successfully.

Create checkpoints for yourself along your path to achieve smaller goals along the way. You can keep yourself motivated to run for a further five minutes or till the end of the block by just looking forward to a prominent landmark along the route, such as a notable tree or statue. This can be an easy way to keep yourself moving forward.

Create your aid station to store supplies and use as a destination point while running on a route you designed yourself rather than one in a park or on an official running course. It will help if you run a circuit or an out-and-back path that takes you from your house (the starting point) to your vehicle (the halfway point) and back to your home (the objective), where you can check in.

You might arrange for a companion to meet you halfway through your run at a spot that has been decided.

Converting a distance objective, such as "I want to run 10 miles today," into a time goal, such as "I want to run 120 minutes today," or vice versa, is another helpful mental strategy for runners.

If your next objective is located 3 miles away, you can mentally prepare yourself by telling yourself, "That's only a half-hour away. "It would be beneficial if you made an effort to refrain from constantly checking your watch or the app that you have open to see how far you have gone in your workout. To avoid the "watched pot never boils" error, put your phone aside after you hit the treadmill's "start" button and concentrate entirely on your workout.

3. Accept the Obstacles with Open Arms

While you're out there logging the kilometers on your long run, remind yourself that training for a long-distance event isn't easy. If it were that easy, wouldn't every single person do it? You've chosen to take on a challenge, and the challenges you face will ultimately make the accomplishment you attain even more rewarding.

When traveling across several miles, keep in mind that you are free to travel at whatever pace is comfortable for you and that you should. Long distances require endurance more than speed. Therefore you should slow down if you find that you are having trouble moving forward. Run at a rate that allows your body to recover, take a break to walk around, or even stop running and sit down for a few minutes if that's what your body requires. Continue once you've collected your thoughts and regained your composure.

4. Find a Mantra as Step Four

While you are jogging, it can be helpful to pick a simple phrase, such as "One step at a time," and repeat it to yourself again in your brain. This will help you keep focused and grounded. It has the potential to serve as your drive whenever you require it the most. Research running mantras and marathon quotes if you don't already have a favorite phrase that you use as a mantra. If you don't, you can use them as inspiration to create your own.

5. Use Imagery to Help Your Mental Toughness

Visualizing yourself as a world-class athlete about to cross the finish line might be helpful when you find yourself in a challenging circumstance. For example, imagine you are in a race's home stretch. Imagine that you are jogging in a fluid, graceful, and calm manner. If you want to imagine yourself crossing the finish line, grabbing the finisher's medal, or even just getting to the next mile marker, apply visualization techniques developed for athletes. Imagine that you are the same runner as someone you greatly respect and think about how you would run if you were them.

6 Engage in Some Counting Games

If you want to run in areas with a lot of other runners, you should try this game. Choose a particular piece of clothing, like a white running helmet, to keep an eye out for a while you are out on your run. After that, make a tally of how many runners you observe sporting it.

When running near or by other runners, keep in mind that you are a part of a community, and allow the connection you all share to inspire and motivate you. You may also do this with cars of a particular make or color if you do a lot of running on the roads. But, again, this is something to consider if you run a lot. Are you going to go through a well-known hiking trail? You might want to try maintaining a record of the different kinds of trees or the number of other animals you come across.

7. Make Post-Run Plans

It is a good idea to plan what you want to do when you finish a run, mainly if you run in the morning. This approach is especially true if you run on an empty stomach. Think about something simple, like deciding what you will eat for dinner. It makes it easier to manage your day and provides something to look forward to once you finish your workout. Should I pace myself according to time or distance?

8. Visualize Your Race

When you are getting ready for a race like a marathon, you should try to picture yourself running the entire course, including each mile, and finishing the competition. This will help you mentally acclimate to the competition. Your mental preparation for the race will be aided by doing this. Think of how you would like to strike a stance for the picture you will take as you cross the finish line. Make an effort to view the clock with your target time displayed (if you have one). Just try to place yourself in the position of a race participant as a volunteer hangs the medal you won around your neck. Think about how it will feel to look back and see your loved ones cheering for you as you cross the finish line. It will be an incredible feeling. Is This a Warning That You Need to Cut Back on Your Running, or Is It Just the Normal Pain That Comes With Working Out Your Muscles?

9 Listen With Your Ears

Put on some headphones throughout your long runs if you want to increase the amount of aural inspiration you get from them. Even though certain officially sanctioned events prohibit the use of headphones or ear-buds on the course, embracing distractions and finding encouragement during your runs by wearing headphones responsibly and exercising prudence may be a rewarding experience. Do you find that you move more while music is playing? Is listening to podcasts a distraction from what you're currently doing? Do you find that listening to audiobooks helps you picture the scenes? While you're out on your runs, try various audio tracks to determine which ones work best for you.

Consider utilizing numerous forms of media if your run is going to be at least an hour long. Start your warm-up kilometers with a podcast, then when you're ready to start picking up the pace, switch to music on your headphones. Perhaps you run without music for the duration of the run and only crank up the volume of your playlist once you reach a plateau in your performance. A good pair of headphones designed for running, along with music or other audio to listen to while you're out on your long runs, can make all the difference.

10. Deep breaths

Long-distance running places a premium on developing good respiratory mechanics. Working on your breathing can assist you in getting the oxygen that your muscles require so that you can run longer distances and increase your endurance. During your training, practice a variety of different breathing techniques. When jogging for extended periods, the most effective breathing method is to take breaths in via the nose and exhale through the mouth. If you're having difficulties maintaining a steady breath, you could slow down and try to time your inhales and exhales with the strike of your foot. Inhale deeply each time your left foot makes contact with the ground. Exhale as you strike the ground with your right foot.

11. Explore an Alternative Running Path

If you decide to train for a long-distance race like a marathon, there is a reasonable probability that you will run the same course during your entire training cycle. Selecting a different path is an excellent way to stave against monotony and boredom while keeping you on your toes. You might run a new route, take a brief detour on your usual route, and discover a new part of the neighborhood. You may keep your mind sharp by deviating from your regular schedule and altering the distance and pace of your long runs.

The mental fortitude required to complete a half marathon is on par with the physical fitness needed to complete the race. Because each stage of the race brings its own distinct set of mental challenges, it would be helpful if you were prepared for the mental games that you might play with yourself when your body starts to tire.

The following is a list of some advice that can assist you in conquering the mental challenges and distractions that arise at each mile of a half marathon.

First 5 Miles:

Begin with a Calm Pace

You will most likely feel power and assurance as you begin your half marathon. You may have to convince yourself to hold back. Because you've trained to run 13.1 miles, you should find the first few miles rather unchallenging. The trick to finishing a half marathon in a thoughtful and enjoyable manner is to run the first half of the race at a slower speed than the pace you run at the second half of the race (this is known as a negative split). Take it easy and try not to worry over anything. After a certain amount of miles, your body will begin to recognize the value of the effort that you have put forth.

Conduct Your Very Own Half Marathon

There is no reason to feel threatened even if there is a large crowd moving around you at the moment. It would be beneficial for you to keep the fable of the tortoise and the hare in your mind at all times. One of the runners' most common and costly errors is starting too quickly. Taking numerous slow, deep breaths and concentrating on your breathing can help prevent your mind from wandering to the other runners competing in the race. You'll get them later when it's convenient for you and at your speed.

Take Care Not to Get Too Emotional

Maintain as much composure as you can for the first five miles of the race. When you see family and friends shouting for you, resist the impulse to give high-fives to fans or jump up and down when you see them. Try to save as much mental energy as possible for the race. Between Miles 6 and 10, the going may become quite complex. During the middle portion of the race, when you run at a tempo pace, your mental toughness will begin to be tested in earnest. However, if you are running a strategic race, it is possible that you won't start to "feel it" until mile 9 or 10, depending on how far you have to go.

When you find yourself going through moments in which you are uncomfortable and questioning your abilities, resist the urge to give in. Don't forget all the kilometers you ran and the hard work you put in at the gym. Believe in the value of your training. Consider how much effort you've put in so far and how satisfying it will be to finish the half marathon you've been training for. It will be beneficial for you to arm yourself with tactics for keeping your mental toughness and then have those strategies ready. This will help you retain your mental toughness.

Break It Up

After you've completed the sixth mile of the race, you should begin to divide the remaining distance into progressively smaller chunks. The space will appear to be less overwhelming and easier to overcome as a result of this. Consider a statement like, "I've completed more than a third of the task!" as an illustration. At mile

10, you should be able to tell yourself, "There's only a short five-kilometer run left to go."

Conquer Your Laziness

Now is the moment to practice all of the strategies you learned to combat boredom while running those long distances in training. Try everything you can to prevent your thoughts from wandering. Find ways to alleviate your boredom that are effective for you personally.

Listed below are some ideas to consider:

Counting your breaths or steps might be a beneficial distraction while trying to focus on anything else.

The act of counting can be similar to meditation in that it can take one's mind off any discomfort felt in the body.

To begin, you should count each step you take in conjunction with your breaths.

First, take a breath in for the count of four, then let it out for the same time.

Do the calculation in your head.

It is beneficial to take your mind off any discomfort you might feel by calculating the square footage of your living room, practicing long division in your head, or reciting multiplication tables. These are all fantastic strategies to distract yourself. Focus on your technique. Run through a mental checklist of technique corrections to correct your form, such as rolling your shoulders down and relaxing your hands, and easing the stiffness in your face. This will help you fix your condition. This will help you practice appropriate forms.

Meditate.

Concentrate on the sound of your breathing or your footsteps to clear your mind. If you make it a habit to meditate while you run in the weeks leading up to your race, you will become more skilled at the practice and will also find it much simpler to empty your mind of distracting thoughts. Mindfulness training should be done.

Establish a goal for yourself regarding what you hope to achieve by completing the half marathon before the start of the competition. Then, as soon as you cross the mile 6 mark, focus on the objective you set for yourself and how you respect that intention as you continue your journey.

Appreciate the body you're in.

Focus your attention on the muscles being worked during your run to get a sense of your strength and power as you move through each region of the body.

Sing.

Listen to some of your favorite music while you run, and let the sound of your feet striking the ground serve as a backbeat for the music.

Have conversations with other runners.

At this stage of the competition, you can encourage your fellow runners by calling out encouraging welcomes or cheering them on (it doesn't matter if the other runners don't talk back). Remember to give yourself some credit and congratulate yourself every time. Take some time to reflect on everything you've accomplished recently. Maintaining a happy attitude is the best course of action for you!

Miles 11 to 13.1: Get Outside Your Body

During the last few miles of the run, you will most likely start to experience an increase in the amount of physical discomfort. You're going to be worn out at the very least. Your lungs will feel like they are on fire, your legs will feel heavy, and your muscles may start to cramp up.

It's possible that these miles will feel particularly challenging if you didn't pace yourself correctly at the beginning of the race.

Try not to be overly critical of oneself.

Instead, it would help if you directed your attention away from your body. Give your attention back to the outside world. Take in the atmosphere by observing the crowd as they cheer, reading the placards they hold, making mental notes on the other runners, and taking in the surrounding landscape.

Talk to Your Mind

The time to pass other runners has arrived at this point in the race. You are going to have to find some additional strength if you want to be able to run the final 5k at the same speed as the race. During your training runs, repeat the running mantras that you have created for yourself. Remember the strategies you've used to push through fatigue during training (and that you can do it again). Remember the goals you want to accomplish, the sacrifices you made, and the feelings you expect to feel after the task is completed.

Set Small Milestones

Keep your attention on the runner in front of you. Push through the pain and get ahead of that runner. When you have successfully past that person, proceed to the subsequent runner and repeat the previous step.

To Conclude, with Force

As the finish line approaches, focus on the present moment and give everything you've got to the race. You may wish to sprint in the final three to six minutes of the race; this decision will be based on your running style. Put some effort into pumping your legs, take a deep breath, and try to quicken the pace of your heartbeat. Consider the race a battle between you and your personal best time, which may help you stay focused. When you get within a half-mile of the finish line, you should start to think of it as competition versus the other runners. This may help alleviate some of the anxiety involved with taking part in a running marathon for specific individuals.

Just Soak It All Up

You will want to recall the accomplishments you have accomplished and the highs you are currently experiencing as you finish strong. As you near the end of the race, bring your thoughts back into focus and give yourself permission to observe, listen to, and experience what is occurring around you.

Mental Recuperation Following the Race

Spend some time after the race perfecting your post-race recovery techniques. Put on your finisher's shirt with pride, examine the medal you just received, and then take stock of how you are currently feeling. Take a minute to allow yourself to feel the feelings you are experiencing, especially if you had been expecting a better time or are dissatisfied with your performance in the race. It would help if you took a 15-minute break to walk off the race.

After you've had some time to process those sensations and clear your head, bring your attention back to the goals you set for yourself. Recognize the strength and power that you displayed through your race. The time has come to celebrate with one's family and close friends. Share your reflections on how you finished the race and what you were able to take away from the experience.

The Blues after the Marathon

There is a possibility that finishing a race will immediately leave you feeling elated, but there is also the possibility that you will experience a post-run low. In the week following a marathon, it is usual for runners to experience feelings of tiredness and depression. Being a marathon runner might make this a common occurrence in your life. Be sure you are anticipating it and have a plan for it.

After a race, you may have post-race blues, but as long as you take care of yourself and give yourself time to recuperate, these feelings should subside within a week or two. You should not delay getting medical attention if the symptoms do not decrease. The chemical changes in your body and brain that could have pushed you over the edge into a clinically severe depression can be reversed if the condition is recognized in its early stages and treated.

Notes on Precaution

Always observe the posted signs for the route and any on-route refreshment and nutrition stops when participating in any organized race, including a half marathon. This includes always making sure to obey the posted signage. At several of the water stations, there will also be a tent with medical personnel standing by to assist you and a restroom for those times when you need to take a quick pause to use the bathroom.

Large organized races will typically have safety designations and a color-coded event warning system, which will denote whether danger levels are low (green), moderate (yellow), high (red), or extreme. In addition, this system will indicate the danger level as either low, medium, high, or severe (black). The rating for each race will be determined based on several factors, including the weather, the state of the road, and other elements. Pay close attention to the conditions outside, the path in front of you, and the level of effort you feel you are putting up while you are running.

At any time throughout the race, if you feel pain or suspect that you may have been injured, you should immediately stop running and make your way to the nearest medical tent for treatment. If you're experiencing cramps while jogging or finding it challenging to keep up with the pace of the other runners, don't be afraid to slow down or stop and walk. The accomplishment of running a half marathon is one of those things that stays with you for the rest of your life, and all the hard work you put into training can pay off on race day.

Recall the importance of keeping your body and mind in sync as you prepare for your race by adhering to your pre-race hydration and feeding plans. When you have completed the 13.1 kilometers, crossed the finish line, and been awarded your medal, you can take comfort in the fact that you are now a half-marathoner for the rest of your life.

BELA CORRIDA
28
Marisa Barros
DOURO

CHAPTER 13

How to Effectively Train to Run a 5K for Beginners

This 5K training program lasts six weeks and is for novice runners or run/walkers who want to work their way up to competing in a 5K (3.1 miles) road race. This fitness routine starts with a run/walk structure and gradually shifts into a running-only format throughout its entirety. When you start, you should already have some real experience with running, and you should also be in good health.

When you've completed the training program, you'll be prepared to compete in a 5K race if that's what you want to do, or you'll have the self-assurance of knowing that you can run a distance of three miles nonstop without stopping. You can also anticipate feeling more powerful and healthier in general. Running consistently, even for a few minutes per day, can help you improve your heart health and even make you live longer.

Why Should You Follow a Training Plan for a 5K?

If you've never participated in a 5K race before, the idea of jogging nonstop for three miles may strike fear into your heart. You could put on your running shoes, go for a jog several times a week, gradually increase the distance you run, and work toward the goal of running 3.1 miles in the future. However, an organized training plan might help you achieve that objective by breaking it down into smaller, more manageable chunks.

The strategy calls for you to gradually increase the time you spend running each week while simultaneously decreasing the time you spend walking throughout the intervals. After six weeks, you can complete a 5K race distance without taking walking breaks. (However, if you prefer to take walking breaks during the race, you are more than welcome to do so.)

Your level of exertion will progressively rise as you progress through the training program to minimize boredom and exhaustion. You will put yourself in challenging situations, but they won't be so complicated that they seem overpowering. In addition, it provides many opportunities for relaxation and rehabilitation, helping your body maintain vitality and strength.

How to Make Use of a Training Plan for a 5K

Even though this routine is intended for novices, you should avoid using it if you haven't exercised for at least three months because it won't be effective. You should ideally be able to run continuously for at least five minutes before beginning this training program. Before attempting the 5K distance, you should first complete a one-mile running program that lasts for four weeks if you are a beginner and have never run before.

Learn the fundamentals of crucial training tenets, such as cross training, recovery days, interval training, and self-evaluation, before beginning your program. You will notice that different types of workouts are recommended for you to undertake on specific days by your training program. Cross training is a term that refers to performing a variety of different forms of exercise in addition to jogging.

Cross Training Exercises

Cross-training can consist of anything other than running that you enjoy doing, such as cycling, yoga, swimming, or any other sport. Regarding overall health and fitness, the American College of Sports Medicine suggests performing strength training anywhere from twice to three times per week. But, again, this is something that runners may benefit from. Studies have indicated that runners who engage in regular resistance training see gains in their muscular strength, running economy, and muscle power, as well as improved performance in the running up to a distance of 10 kilometers.

Intervals

Short spurts of increased exertion are referred to as intervals in the sport of running. Runners occasionally push themselves to their limits by engaging in speed or hill intervals to improve their overall performance. In addition, it teaches runners how to adapt their efforts and paces to different situations. According to several studies, sprint interval training is an efficient approach for trained athletes to improve both their endurance and their power. Interval training may appear more complex than other types of workouts, but including intervals in your routine not only adds diversity but also helps prevent monotony.

Rest Days

Your training schedule should include both running days and days dedicated to rest and recovery. Taking breaks during the week allows your body and mind to recuperate and refresh. As a result, you have a responsibility to make sure that you allow yourself the necessary amount of time each week to recover.

When reviewing the weekly plan, make any necessary adjustments to your schedule. You are not required to complete your runs on particular days; however, you should try to avoid running back-to-back days whenever possible.

Either completely relax for one day in between runs, or engage in some other form of physical activity.

Taking Stock of Your Development

As you progress through the program, pay attention to how you are feeling overall. Be mindful of both your current levels of energy and your capacity to maintain a regular exercise schedule.

On a particular week, you can perform the workouts more than once before moving on to the following week in the program if you feel it is moving too rapidly. This may require you to push back the date of your 5K race (if you signed up for one). However, rescheduling the event might be more prudent if you push yourself to the brink of fatigue or injury to stay on time.

Try a 6-week intermediate 5K training schedule if you feel as though this workout routine is too easy for you. You could even feel ready to step up your game with a more advanced training schedule for the 5K. Use a pace calculator to keep track of your improvement as you go through your workout routine and observe how much stronger you are becoming.

5K Workout Plan for the First Week

Day 1: On this day, you should run for 5 minutes, then walk for 1 minute. Iterate this training method three times.

Day 2: consists of either rest or cross-training.

Day 3: On this day you will run for six minutes and walk for one minute. Iterate this training method three times.

Day 4: This day will be a time to relax and recuperate.

Day 5: You should run for 7 minutes and then walk for 1 minute. Iterate this training routine three times.

Day 6 is a rest day or a cross-training day.

Day 7: This day will be a time to rest.

Week 2

Day 1: On this day you will run for 7 minutes and then stroll for 1 minute. Iterate this training routine three times.

Day 2 consists of either rest or cross-training.

Day 3: You should run for 8 minutes and then walk for 1 minute. After that, sprint as hard as you can for one minute, and then walk for two minutes. Do this three times. To finish, you will run for 7 minutes and then walk for 1 minute.

Day 4: This day will be a time to relax and recuperate.

Day 5: You should run for 9 minutes and then walk for 1 minute.

Iterate this training method three times.

Day 6 is a rest day or a cross-training day.

Day 7: This day will be a time to rest.

Week 3

Day 1: You should run for 10 minutes, then walk for 1 minute. It would help if you repeated this training routine two times.

Day 2: On this day, focus on circuit training.

Day 3: You should run for 12 minutes and then walk for 1 minute. After that, sprint as hard as you can for one minute, and then stroll for two minutes.

This training routine should be done four times.

Day 4: This day will be a time to rest.

Day 5: On day five, you will run for 13 minutes and then stroll for 1 minute. This training routine should be repeated twice.

Day 6: is a rest day or a cross-training day.

Day 7: This day will be a day to relax and recuperate.

Week Four

Day 1: You should run for 15 minutes and then walk for 1 minute.

It would help if you repeated this training routine twice.

Day 2 focuses on circuit training.

Day 3: You should run for 17 minutes and then walk for 1 minute. After that, add two more intervals in which you will run at a high intensity for one minute and then stroll for two minutes.

Day 4: This will be a day to relax and recuperate.

Day 5: You should run for 19 minutes, walk for 1 minute and then run for 7 minutes.

Day 6 is a rest day or a cross-training day.

Day 7: This will be a day to relax and recuperate.

Week 5

Day 1: You should run for 20 minutes, walk for 1 minute, and then run for 6 minutes.

Day 2 focuses on circuit training.

Day 3: You should run for 15 minutes and then walk for 1 minute. After that, sprint as hard as you can for one minute, and then stroll for two minutes. Repeat this training routine three times.

Day 4: This will be a day of rest.

Day 5: Run for a total of 26 minutes on this day.

Day 6 is a rest day or a cross-training day.

Day 7: This will be a day to relax and recuperate.

Week Six

Day 1: You should run for 20 minutes and then walk for 1 minute. After that, sprint as hard as you can for one minute, and then stroll for two minutes. This training routine will be repeated twice.

Day 2: This day consists of either rest or cross-training.

Day 3: Run for half an hour on day 3.

Day 4: This is a day to relax and recuperate.

Day 5: On this day, do a twenty-minute run.

Day 6: Rest.

Day 7: Race day!

Getting Ready for a Five Kilometer Race

After you have finished a training program for a 5K, you can consider taking part in a 5K race or a fun run to celebrate your accomplishment. It's even possible that you have one already penciled in on your calendar. It is helpful to plan to feel as good as possible on the day of the event.

Conditions: When you can, try to train in situations that are similar to the way you work out on a race day. If the starting time of your event is set for the early morning, you should also plan some of your training runs for the early morning so that your body can become used to running at that hour of the day. Determine the type of pre-race feeding that is most effective for you and use it.

You don't want stomach problems on race day because that could ruin your experience. Therefore, during your training, try out a variety of pre-run snacks and beverages, and then employ one of those strategies on race day.

You should use equipment that is comfortable for you to use. On race day, you should not be testing any new running gear or footwear. It would help if you started getting ready for the race the night before by laying out your most comfortable running clothes and best pair of running shoes, as well as your bib number and any food or drinks that you intend to bring with you to the starting line. The next morning, when you wake up on race day, you'll have fewer things to worry about, and you'll be able to dedicate your attention to running a fantastic time.

It is in your best interest to educate yourself on what to anticipate from road races if this is your first time participating. It would help if you directed any inquiries about the race to the person who organized it. It is also beneficial to participate in other races in the area before the one in question, both to gain experience and to observe and interact with other runners.

Try your hand at either a novice 10K training program or a beginner half marathon training program if you feel like you're ready for the next step in your athletic journey.

Your preparations for your first 5K race are finally over, and the big day has arrived. Congratulations! It is very typical to experience some pre-race nerves or to question what to anticipate on the day of the race. Examine some of the do's and don'ts for the days leading up to the event, as well as for the race day itself, to help you feel more at ease as you make your way to the starting line of your first 5K. This will enable you to feel more prepared and confident as you run.

Should you get in any workout the day before a 5K?

In this situation, no answer is correct or incorrect. To provide their muscles with the necessary rest before a competition, many runners opt to take a day off from running to relax and unwind before the race. They report that when they get to the starting line, they feel revitalized and prepared for the race. Some runners, particularly those who are more easily anxious, believe that going for a very slow jog for twenty minutes the day before a race is the best way to prepare themselves mentally and physically for the competition.

To avoid feeling weary or hurting the next day, avoid working out for an extended period or in a manner that is overly strenuous. Could you keep it simple and keep it brief? Don't bother trying to cram for the test because you won't be able to get any fitter or quicker in the week leading up to the 5K you're running.

1. DON'T: Get your fill of carbohydrates the night before.

When people hear that runners consume a lot of carbohydrates before a primary race, they sometimes assume that this advice should be followed before running any event.

If you are running a race of a longer distance, such as a half or full marathon, you will only require additional carbohydrates.

It is unnecessary to consume many carbohydrates the day before a 5K event if you plan on jogging. Eat the same things you would typically eat the day before the race, but try to stay away from items that are particularly oily or fatty, as these can cause problems in the digestive tract.

The present moment is not the right time to try out unusual dishes or cuisines.

2. DO: Gather your race supplies as soon as possible.

If possible, pick up your race bib, timing chip (if the race uses them), and goodie bag the day before the event. This will ensure that you have everything you need. As a result, you won't be rushed on race day to get a T-shirt and will have a higher chance of acquiring your preferred size.

3. DO: Prepare your clothes for the race.

You must examine the weather in the days leading up to the race to ensure that you are well-prepared to handle any circumstances, including severe heat, cold, or even rain. Dress as though it is 15 degrees warmer outside; this is a good rule of thumb. When you start running, you'll feel that much warmer in that amount of time. If it is chilly, you can always choose to dress more warmly while you are waiting for the race to begin. A gear check is a service that is offered at many different events. You can leave your luggage with spare clothes there before and after the race.

Prepare everything you need for the next day's activities the night before so that you won't have to scramble and rush around in the morning. "Nothing new on race day," as the saying goes, is the most crucial rule about what you should wear for your 5K. It is not the moment to test out your brand-new pair of running shoes or your newest adorable attire. Prepare for the race by donning the same tried-and-true running attire that you've used in the past. This will help you avoid unexpected pain or problems, such as chafing or blistering.

As a result, the free race T-shirt you receive when picking up your bib is generally not something you want to wear. However, you can get it when you pick up your race packet. The T-shirts worn during the race are often made of cotton, which, when wet from sweat, can become cumbersome and uncomfortable. In addition, many competitors believe putting on the shirt before completing the race brings ill luck.

4. DO: Get an excellent night's sleep

It is normal to feel anxious in the hours leading up to the start of the race, even if this is not the first time you have participated in a competitive event. In the days preceding your race, you should limit yourself to soothing things, such as reading a book or watching a movie. In addition to that, you must receive a sufficient amount of sleep. Even if you know that falling asleep or staying asleep would be difficult, you need to get off your feet and get some shuteye as soon as possible. You cannot afford to wait.

5. Make sure you eat breakfast.

On the morning of the race, you don't want to overeat, but you also don't want to compete with a stomach that is empty. Keeping this in mind, make sure you choose your pre-race meal carefully.

Eat something light, such as a snack or small meal, at least one hour before the start of the race so that your stomach will be less likely to become upset. During the marathon, having a full stomach may cause you to have cramping or side stitches. Avoid foods that are dense, high in fat, or have a high fiber content because these can induce gastrointestinal problems.

6. DO: Get there early for the race.

Before the race, you must make sure that you leave yourself plenty of time to find a good parking area, pick up your bib number (if you haven't already), check your bag, and use the restroom (the lines may be extended).

If you have negative thoughts before the race or while competing, make an effort to concentrate on nothing but your breathing and run the race as if you couldn't care less about the result.

Make the most of your time by keeping in mind that the only person you are competing against is yourself, and remember to do your best.

7. DO: Warm-up before getting ready for the race

When competing in a shorter event, such as a 5K, it is essential to perform a warm-up to gradually elevate your heart rate and make your muscles ready to serve. Do a slow jog for approximately five to ten minutes, about fifteen minutes before the start of the race, and then walk quickly to the starting line.

8. DO: Fasten your bib on your shirt.

Please ensure the race's bib is displayed prominently on the front of your shirt, and secure it with a safety pin in each of the four corners. Typically, you may acquire one of these at the exact location where you pick up your bib. It is proper racing etiquette to display your bib at the front rather than the back of your jersey. Doing so also alerts race officials to the fact that you are taking part in the competition.

If there are official race photographers on the route, they will also use your bib number to identify the images they take of you throughout the race. Therefore, you should ensure that your number can be easily seen, particularly at the finish line. If there is a B-Tag timing device attached to the back of your race bib, check to see that it is not bent and that it is not covered by any articles of clothing or a running belt.

Things You Ought to Remember: At the Beginning, Get in Line

It would help if you weren't too close to the front at the starting line. At the beginning of the race, faster and more experienced runners prefer not to go around novice runners, who are likely to move at a slower pace. In specific competitions, runners are divided into corrals or given post-race instructions based on their predicted pace. If not, ask other runners in the area about their planned pace. You should back up further if it's faster than your pace.

If you're surrounded by people who move at the same speed, settling into your rhythm will be much simpler. It may feel congested at the beginning of the race; however, as the race progresses, the crowd will thin out, and you will quickly be able to find your groove.

9. DO NOT: Exit the building too quickly

Even for experienced runners, this is a common pitfall in the racing world. The exhilaration and anticipation of the start of the race may push practically all of the runners to get off to a far faster start than they had initially intended. This speed might feel nice at first, but it could end up costing you in the long run. Maintain command of the situation by keeping tabs on your pace early on.

10. Make Use of All of the Water Stops

Make use of the water stations that are scattered around the route. They are available to help you out! If you've never gotten water from a hydration stop before, the following instructions should help you get it right the first time. Also, don't forget to show the volunteers that aided you some appreciation for their efforts in passing out the water!

Bring along any members of your support group. Send out invitations to your loved ones, including your friends and family, to come to see you compete. To make it easier for you to push yourself in the end, you should ask them to stand near the finish line.

11. Have fun!

When competing in your first 5K race, try not to put too much pressure on yourself to finish in a rapid time. A first-time participant's goal should be to complete the race successfully and to take pleasure in the event. Pat yourself on the back, and savor the rush of excitement that comes with crossing the finish line for the first time.

Congratulations on achieving one of the goals you set for yourself, which was to finish your first 5K race, and I want to take this opportunity to wish you continued success in all of your future endeavors. We wish you a successful running journey from the starting line to the finish, thanks to these helpful hints I have discovered in my thirty years of running. We'll be waiting for you when you're ready to take on the next challenge so you can bask in your success (and your new personal record for the 5K) in the meantime.

XX Milha Riberinha
da Baixa da Banheira
445
ATLETISMOITA

CONCLUSION

Running is a physical activity that can be performed at any time, in any location, and does not require buying expensive equipment. You can even do it right in front of your own home. The only necessities are training clothes and a reliable pair of running shoes, but the payoff in improved physical and mental health is immense.

Despite the allure of this activity, getting started with running can be challenging. Fear is one of the key reasons why many people don't go for their first run. The good news is that you can take practical steps to reduce your worries, which can inspire you to start running (and experiencing all those beneficial side effects).

It is possible to begin and maintain motivation in a running program by undergoing a mental shift, selecting conscious actions, and understanding how to refrain from comparing oneself to other runners. Running on top of everything else you already have in your life might be challenging. It is possible that incorporating this new habit into your routine will feel overwhelming to you. If you feel intimidated, remember that this is a natural reaction, especially when you are beginning something completely fresh. Even if you only run for ten minutes each day, you could see a significant improvement in the quality of your life. This matter is factual, even if taking up the challenge proves complicated.

You will need a lot of time to overcome your anxiety about running. Still, you may immediately start improving your self-confidence by performing a few basic behaviors. The best method to begin building confidence in your abilities to run is to engage in activities such as talking walks, practicing self-regulation of negative thoughts, and actively seeking encouragement from the significant people in your life.

Running can help you improve your energy levels, your mood, and the quality of sleep you get, in addition to lowering the risk of developing chronic health conditions. Having little energy is cited by many runners as one of the primary factors contributing to their inability to run as regularly as they would like to. Your best efforts to maintain a steady running regimen can be derailed by chronic weariness. And besides, when your body is exhausted, it is difficult to muster the enthusiasm to get out of bed and test the boundaries of your abilities. Therefore, what can you do to boost your energy levels so that you have the desire to walk or run more frequently? Modifications to one's lifestyle, even minor ones, can significantly impact. It's possible that you already participate in some of these healthy activities; nevertheless, if you can practice a few more of them, you may find that you gain a spring in your step, which increases your running program. If this is the case, then congratulations!

Maintaining healthy eating habits and getting enough sleep are other essential parts of your overall well-being plan. An individual runner's diet will differ, but it should include a variety of macronutrients, complex carbohydrates, and plant-based micronutrients. Because of the body's capacity to rapidly break down carbohydrates during periods of intensive physical exercise, carbohydrates are the preferred fuel source for runners. Runners should consume a carb and protein-rich post-workout snack to refuel their muscles and prevent muscular fatigue.

Running is beneficial for both the mind and the body and has several benefits. It can help you maintain a healthy weight, protect your bones and cognitive function, and increase your self-esteem and sense of community. In addition, you can still receive the benefits of running even if you do it once per week, and you can always build up to running for longer distances and more frequently throughout your running career.

Running is a terrific activity for getting exercise, fresh air, and discovering new parts of your neighborhood. If you find that running outside is something you enjoy doing, there is no reason you can't keep doing it throughout the year. You may still enjoy running even when the weather is hot, chilly, humid, or wet as long as you plan.

Be aware that even the most accomplished runners can avoid injury by planning time for rest and incorporate other types of training. On days when you cross-train, choose activities with lesser impact, such as swimming or cycling, so that you may recover and give your running muscles vacation from their hard work. Talk to your physician if you are unsure how often you should exercise or if it is safe for you to start running if you don't already do so. They can provide you with a recommendation for a physical fitness program suitable for your current age and fitness level.

Running is beneficial on many levels for people of all ages and levels of physical fitness. You can enhance your overall health, prolong your longevity, maintain healthy body composition, increase your cognitive ability, and improve your mental health. Talking with your primary care physician before commencing a new exercise plan is crucial. This is of utmost importance if you have a debilitating ailment that requires ongoing treatment, such as arthritis or heart disease.

You probably already know this, but pounding the pavement can put a significant amount of strain on your body. Your training could be hampered by an injury, like a runner's knee or shin splints. Even worse, there is a possibility that you will be required to miss the first stage of a tournament that you have been training for many months. Suppose you experience pain that has persisted for more than seven to ten days. In that case, you need to schedule an appointment with a medical professional so that they may investigate the potential reasons for your condition and provide a treatment plan for you.

When you first start running, you shouldn't worry too much about your pace or distance; just getting out there and running or engaging in any other type of physical activity is a step in the right direction. Discovering the drive that will propel you forward is the most crucial step. Inexperienced runners frequently lack clarity over how to set goals for their speed and distance properly. If you are starting as a runner, you might wonder whether you should focus on increasing your speed or your distance during your training. The quick response is that you should focus on your distance training first.

When starting your running program, it is recommended that you begin by constructing a foundation of endurance. That indicates that you should first work on increasing your aerobic fitness. You decide to up your mileage to make longer distances easier for your body. Your speed will improve in tandem with your increased endurance as you train.

You can train simultaneously for both distances and speed once you have built up some of the muscle and endurance necessary to finish the workout. Then, having built up some strength and endurance for completing the distance, you can train simultaneously for both distances and speed. If you alternate between longer, slower runs and shorter, more intense sessions, it can help you can get the most from your workout while reducing the risk of injury at the same time. This training method can be accomplished by simply varying your schedule.

Dehydrated athletes are more likely to experience weariness, headaches, poor coordination, nausea, and muscle cramps. The prevention of heat-related disorders, such as heat stroke, which can have severe repercussions, depends on maintaining an adequate hydration level. In addition to all those unpleasant sensations, dehydration also makes you move more slowly.

According to one study's findings, a runners' performance was negatively affected even by a "modest decrement in hydration status" on a hot day. The most detailed information now available for runners to stay hydrated is to aim to drink only when thirsty. Drinking water when you are thirsty can help prevent both underhydration, which can lead to dehydration, and overhydration, which can lead to hyponatremia. Both of these health conditions can be avoided by drinking water when thirsty. The findings of this investigation are backed up by evidence from the scientific community (low blood salt levels due to abnormal fluid retention).

When drinking fluids while running, the basic rule of thumb is to consume between 4 and 6 ounces of fluid every 20 minutes. The American College of Sports Medicine recommends that runners who are sustaining a pace that is faster than 8 minutes per mile drink 6 to 8 ounces of liquids every 20 minutes. When working out for extended periods (at least 90 minutes), you should replace the sodium and other minerals you lose by drinking a sports drink as part of your fluid intake.

So you've opted to go for a run. Congrats! You have just completed the first stage of your training to become a runner. It doesn't matter if you're a weekend warrior or a professional marathoner; the journey begins with the simple resolve to keep putting one foot in front of the other. Then, after you've finished your run for the day, make it a point to celebrate! It is not a simple chore to leave the house, nor is it easy to exert yourself physically. Assure yourself that any progress is preferable to none and that you are doing an outstanding job of working toward achieving your goals!

www.ingramcontent.com/pod-product-compliance
Lightning Source LLC
LaVergne TN
LVHW010546160826
845677LV00013B/3019
* 9 7 9 8 8 4 8 3 3 9 3 6 9 *